A WORD IN YOUR EAR

PHILIP HOWARD

A Word in Your Ear

New York
OXFORD UNIVERSITY PRESS
1983

First published in Great Britain 1983
by Hamish Hamilton Ltd
Garden House 57–59 Long Acre London WC2E 9JZ

First published in the United States of America 1983
by Oxford University Press, Inc.

ISBN 0-19-520437-9

Quare habe tibi quicquid hoc libelli,
Qualecumque; quod, o patrona virgo,
Plus uno maneat perenne saeclo.

CONTENTS

INTRODUCTION

I know that you guys are not on a boondoggle in the boondocks, and that if you had your druthers you would be at home today with your loose shoes on. The objective of this introduction is not to basically get down to the nitty-gritties, but to carefully use the one foot in the water approach, and to briefly orchestrate the scenario, big-picturewise, in a concise summarization.

You all know how to fish and cut bait, but don't try to boil the ocean. This ain't a whole new ball game—you have most of the players in place. Hopefully you won't have to lean over backwards to maintain a low profile when you get into bed with your people. However, you may have to open the kimono to get a quick gut feel. Get a handle on the hot buttons before the whole ball of wax becomes a can of worms coming at you from left field. The big grunt is coming and we will all be up to our armpits in alligators—but you can bet your buttocks that that—(expletive deleted) SOB is just shooting from the hip. He's got it all hanging out, and if we go like gangbusters we can blow the whistle on his rip-off without too much moonlighting. His snow-job hasn't got a snowball's chance in Hell, but we can expect a shoot-out because a lot of those rattlesnakes creeping out of the woodwork don't like a womb-to-tomb deal.

Let me run the idea up the flagpole once again. There's an awful lot of that activity going on out there and we can't have any of that rubbernecking. We're between the rock and the hard place. We can't just let the ideas bubble up so that we can wrap them up and fold them in. We have to put on the bells and whistles ourselves even though they are not cast in concrete—so, knife-and-fork a solution, and don't nickel-and-dime the show-stoppers, but let's not have a donneybrook.

My plan is still a bit iffy, but I don't think it's a dog. You can do yourself a favor by biting the bullet and hanging in there. It won't cost an arm and a leg.

The English language is a prolix jungle, rich with exotic blooms of slang, entangled with lianas of jargon and undergrowth of dialect and colloquialism, overshadowed by the great trunks of grammar and vocabulary that have been growing for a thousand years and more. One view (the Tower of Babel version) is that the whole thing has got out of hand, and that the jungle is becoming so impenetrable that by the end of the century inhabitants of its different forests and clearings will be cut off and unable to communicate with each other.

This anxiety that the English language itself is in a period of decline or even decadence suddenly bubbled up in the 1970s. It questioned the marked descriptivism of linguistics since the war. It asked whether *anything* really goes in English; whether all is really for the best in the best of possible words; whether teachers of English had done well to discard so many ideas of 'correct' grammar, usage, spelling, and pronunciation. It manifested itself in regular columns dealing with verbal error in newspapers and magazines around the world, usually, but not invariably, written by amateur wordsmiths rather than professors of linguistics, who were having their private problems with structuralism. This new climate of prescriptivism persuaded even the Editor-in-Chief of the Oxford Dictionaries to begin to add his own opinions about the acceptability of certain words or meanings in educated use in his *Supplement*. Being a modest man as well as a fine scholar, R. W. Burchfield did it in the mildest possible way, explaining (to adapt a statement by John Ray in 1691) that his prescriptions were meant 'as oil to preserve the mucilage from inspissation.' For example, under the new use of 'pre' as a preposition to mean 'before', *Volume III O-Scz* of the *Supplement* cites Henry Kissinger in a Department of State Bulletin: 'Pre my being in office; those decisions were made in the previous Administration.' The Editor glossed this: 'Usually found in contexts where *before* would be equally appropriate and more agreeable.'

That is a remarkable change from the orthodox modern doctrine that lexicographers and other professionals of linguistics are there to describe and explain the language, but never and by no means to prescribe rules about how it should be used.

I got into this in 1975. Anybody who writes for a living is likely to take some interest in the linguistic tools of his or her trade. Some take more than others. Dorothy Parker has the nice image of a

10

woman romantic writer of the Barbara Cartland school, whose words flow easily and in torrents whenever she turns the tap; whereas Proust, poor sap, used to writhe around on the cork floor in agonies to find exactly the word he wanted. In 1975 the West German terrorist, Ulrike Meinhof, shouted at the judge who was trying her: 'You imperialist state-pig.' She actually shouted in German: *'Imperialistische Staatsschwein'*; but it came up on the Reuter's tape in translation. At morning conference at *The Times* my editor, William Rees-Mogg, a man with an agreeable taste for the byways and eccentricities of the news, asked me to write a piece explaining what Frau Meinhof meant by her resounding insult. I did, and have carried on ever since in an occasional column called 'New Words for Old.'

There is a respectable pedigree for articles about the state of the language, stretching from Samuel Johnson and *The Spectator* to the Fowlers, Eric Partridge, Ivor Brown, and their modern epigoni. Anybody who writes seriously sometimes watches himself at work. I think that there is some evidence that Shakespeare himself had the bug. Several of his favourite heroes and heroines are wordsmiths as well as wits, with a deplorable taste for puns and other forms of linguistic introspection.

That original piece about imperialist state-pigs still seems to me reasonably sound; though, if I were writing it again, I think I should pay more attention to the theory of imperialism as a stage in the development of capitalist economy expounded by Communist writers after Lenin. But some of the other articles strike me today as unduly magisterial and priggish.

For instance, I sweat with embarrassment to read the article that I wrote about 'hopefully' in 1975. That was the year when the new absolute use of hopefully, meaning 'it is to be hoped', swept over Britain from across the Atlantic. The analysis and derivations of the new use still stand. The suggestion that it is illiterate seems snobbish. The prediction that it would rapidly fade away, as soon as the novelty had worn off, was a forecast so far-out that it would persuade even a prophet of Baal to give in and take up some less demanding occupation. The statement that it was impossible to distinguish between the absolute 'hopefully' and the adverbial 'hopefully', meaning 'in a hopeful manner', was just wrong.

We have devised our ways of distinguishing between the two. In speech we do it by intonation; in writing we isolate the absolute 'hopefully' with a comma.

11

I gave up fretting about 'hopefully' in the Highlands of Scotland, where, miles from anywhere, and untainted by metropolitan trendiness, an aged shepherd used it in pretty well every other sentence, with a canny Highland accent. The word fills a linguistic need. I do not use it myself. We do not encourage its use in *The Times*. All great word-factories have to have rules, promulgated in the house stylebook; otherwise chaos would reign. But if a good writer used 'hopefully' absolutely and deliberately and in a context where it was appropriate, I should feel uneasy about altering it.

If you want to attack 'hopefully', it is no good saying that it is illiterate, or ungrammatical, or ambiguous, or American, or vulgar. I think that your only line of attack (and not a bad one) is that it is pretentious. It is showing off. It often means no more than 'I hope.'

Much of the anxiety about the language is not so much linguistic as political. People dislike the jargon of the new social sciences because they reveal uncomfortable new truths about the world and themselves. Sociology, psychology, statistics, economics, and the others turn over stones, and we are not always reassured by what crawls out, socially as well as linguistically. Expressions like 'ongoing' and 'right on' and 'relevant' and 'viable' are emblems of the social and political divisions within our society. Linguistic conservatives are fussing, partly anyway, about symptoms not causes of a rapidly changing world.

Accordingly, while Robert Burchfield and other professionals have shifted a little towards prescription, I seem to have shifted a little towards description. People are going to use 'hopefully' how they want, regardless of the prescriptions of prigs. Language does change all the time, as Samuel Johnson recognized when he gave up his ambition to reform the language: 'If the changes that we fear be thus irresistible, what remains but to acquiesce with silence, as in the other insurmountable distresses of humanity? It remains that we retard what we cannot repel, that we palliate what we cannot cure.'

That does not mean that we are completely permissive and relativist and neutral about language. There is good and bad use of English at the diverse levels and for the many purposes that we use it. The wise man pursues the good and eschews the bad. Writers and publishers who do otherwise are sooner or later found out by their contemporaries or by the long eye of history.

Of course there is a lot of junk around: trendy slang like the

efflorescence of the gaudy growth at the beginning of this introduction (though some of it seems to me lively, with the charm of
primitive painters, and all of it is ephemeral); turgid jargon of
specialists; Officialese; Abstractitis; pomposity; and all the other
forms of linguistic flatulence. But it seems to me nonsense to suppose
that English itself is decaying. Good writers and speakers are using
it as well as ever, with far wider jungles of topic and vocabulary
than ever before. True poetry is still being written. In some parts
of the jungle (scholarly books for the general reader, school text-
books in some subjects, fiction, informal conversation by ordinary
people) we are using the language as well as it has ever been used.
Even newspapers, and the rest of the media, attacked by linguistic
conservatives for being sources of the death of English, seem to me
to be doing all right. The cure for dreaming of a golden age, when
English was handled with proper respect, is to go back to the Thirties
and read the press and listen to broadcasts of the time. The language
sounds intolerably stuffy and pedantic and narrow. We do better
today for our brisker world, my masters.

The English language has survived the anxiety of linguistic conservatives and the outrages of linguistic radicals for ten centuries.
It seems to me still to be in rude health, used with elegance and
accuracy, force and majesty by our best writers and speakers from
all over the world.

Until 1980 the average length of tenure of an Editor of *The Times*
was nearer twenty than ten years. In the two years since then we
have had no fewer than three of them. I thank each of them, with
his very disparate interests and talents, for continuing to support
The Times's traditional interest in language and to publish the column
'New Words for Old'. For ideas, correction, education, and laughter
about the delights of English, I thank a noble army of wordsmiths,
and especially: Denis Baron, Francis Bennion, Henry Button, Robert
Burchfield, Sir David Croom-Johnson, Derek Darby, Peter Fellgett,
Gay Firth, Alfred Friendly, Roy Fuller, Hamish Hamilton, John
Harris, Anthony Holden, James Holladay, David Hunt, Elspeth
Huxley, Nicholas Kurti, Bernard Levin, Edwin Newman, John
Newman, Edward Quinn, Anthony Quinton, Randolph Quirk,
Isabel Raphael, William Rees-Mogg, Alan Ross, J. M. Ross, William
Safire, Christopher Sinclair-Stevenson, Peter Stothard, John Sykes,
Philippa Toomey, Laurence Urdang, Laurie Weston; and all other
word children and logophiles who have corresponded with me.

1/ ADULTERY

For adults only

> The mind is guilty of adultery even if it merely pictures to itself a vision of carnal pleasure.
> Lactantius, *Divinae institutiones* VI

In 1980 the Pope denounced lust within marriage as a form of adultery. His suggestion of an eleventh commandment, or at any rate an alarming gloss on the seventh, may be theologically sound, though it makes those outside the Pope's mysteries raise their eyebrows. But it is semantic nonsense. It follows a common and deplorable pattern of blunting the precision of a word by firing it from a blunderbuss instead of a rifle, in the hope of hitting everything in sight. Starvation and mass unemployment are detestable. To describe them as 'obscene' erodes the meaning of 'obscene', without making one's detestation any more emphatic.

Adultery wears its primary meaning on its face. The etymology and shape of the word declare that it means going off to somebody *other* than one's husband, or possibly wife. It comes a winding road, by way of the odd Old French phonetic derivative *avoutrie*, from the past participle stem of the Latin verb *adulterare*, to debauch, corrupt, or commit adultery.

Festus, the grammarian who epitomized *De significatu verborum* (the work of Verrius Flaccus, the most erudite of the Augustan scholars) in the late second century, explained for us: *'adulter et adultera dicuntur quod et ille ad alteram et haec ad alterum se conferunt.'* It is called adultery because one takes oneself off to someone *other* than one's lawful wedded husband. It is evident that Festus is thinking of the two guilty parties to the defilement of a woman's marriage. No pagan writer ever described a husband's betrayal of

14

his own marriage as 'adultery'. Wives committed adultery; husbands had a good time.

But the Christians (or some of them) had no time for the double standard. Lactantius (*Divinae institutiones*, VI, 23) wrote: 'According to secular law, only the wife can be guilty of adultery—when she has another man; the husband, even if he has a number of women, is free from *that* charge. But the divine law so welds two people into matrimony that it is into one flesh, uniting them on equal terms, so that whichever of them sunders the unity of that flesh is guilty of adultery.' St Jerome (*Letters* 77, 3) is equally vigorous, though he does not apply the actual word 'adultery' to the husband's misconduct.

Leaving the early Fathers to get on with it, the strict definition of adultery in English is the voluntary sexual intercourse of a married person with one of the opposite sex, whether unmarried or married to another. The former case is technically described as 'single', the latter as 'double' adultery.

Prophets, theologians, and others in the God-bothering classes bothered by sex, could not leave the simple word alone. It was too useful for condemning abominations and hanky-panky of all sorts. The Pope has eminent predecessors for his misuse of language. When Christ said: 'Whosoever looketh on a woman to lust after her, hath committed *adulterie* with her already in his heart', he was extending the word metaphorically in a spiritually profound, though somewhat daunting way. Others were less careful with their language. Adultery was blunted to mean unchastity generally. Fanatical theologians used the word to describe marriages of which they disapproved, for example of a nun, a widower, or a Christian with a Jew. The Pope's own gloomy apophthegm was found by the ecclesiastical writers of the Middle Ages. For example, 'The too ardent lover of his wife is an adulterer' ('*Adulter est,*' *inquit, 'in suam uxorem amator ardentior'*) appeared in Gratian's *Decretum*, a work of great popularity and influence. The quotation can be traced back to the *Contra Iovinianum* of St Jerome.

In theology this weasel word use is technically called 'interpretative adultery'; in other words, 'let me do the interpreting.'

Adultery was extended in Scripture figuratively to mean the worship of idols. For example, *Jeremiah* III, 9: 'And it came to pass through the lightness of her whoredom, that she defiled the land, and committed adultery with stocks and stones.'

This is a puzzling image for anybody unprepared for the extravagance of scriptural language. I think we can see how it arose. The English meaning of adultery, based ultimately on a Christian definition, differs from the Hebrew notion in one important respect; the same one by which it differed from the pagan notion. In Old Testament law, the sole criterion of adultery is the status of the woman (married or betrothed). A married man having it off with an unmarried, unbetrothed, or divorced woman is not an adulterer in the Old Testament. The prophetic identification of idolatry with adultery derives from the symbolism depicting the Covenant as a marriage between God and the daugher of Zion (see, for example, *Hosea* II or *Ezekiel* XVI). Within such a context, Jeremiah's reference to Israel's adulterous whorings after stocks and stones makes sense, of a sort.

Medieval ecclesiastical writers picked up the strong word to express their loathing for something far worse than any sin of the flesh: doing down a churchman. The enjoyment by an outsider of a benefice during the lifetime of the legal incumbent, or the translation of a bishop from one see to another are both described as adultery by zealous churchmen, rolling their tongues around the word. This kind is technically described, in the jargon, as 'spiritual adultery.'

Again, I think we can see how this arose. It stems ultimately from Chapter V of St Paul's letter to the *Ephesians*, in which Christ's relation to his church is described metaphorically as a form of marriage. In medieval sacramental theology, bishops and priests were seen as Christ's representatives to their respective churches. If each priest stands in the place of Christ to his own church, it is possible, I suppose, to see the priest also as being in the relation of spouse to that church, if you have a taste for such analogies. It was for this reason that the early Fathers frowned on the translation of bishops from one see to another. It may be mystical and metaphysical, but it is not illogical. It was sufficiently important to be the root cause of war between Pope and Emperor in the eleventh century.

In the United States 'adulterated' is commonly used when describing food that has become contaminated, and it is in this sense that it is used in the Federal Food, Drug, and Cosmetic Act. This Act has recently been amended to embrace not only Food, Drugs, and Cosmetics, but also Medical Devices. Thus a piece of medical equipment that does not conform to its specified performance or construction is described, gloomily, as 'adulterated'. British Industry commonly uses the word 'defective' in these circumstances.

16

The Pope's extension of adultery has a long line of precedents for such imprecision. It is not quite adultery, but adulteration of the language.

2/ ANACHRONISM

There is nothing like a date

What's time? Leave Now for dogs and apes:
Man has Forever.
Robert Browning, *A Grammarian's Funeral*, 1855

Anachronism, anachronism, there is nothing like anachronism; it defies the laws of time, and it defies the law of gravity. There is *Schadenfreude* in pointing out anachronism, akin to the instinct that makes one write to journalists pointing out errors in their articles. When Falstaff exclaims, 'Let the sky rain potatoes,' it is agreeable to be able to reply, 'Potatoes haven't been brought back from the New World yet, Fatso.'

When the carrier in *Henry IV Part I* complains that the turkeys in his pannier are quite starved, we know-alls enjoy pointing out that America and therefore turkeys were not discovered until nearly a century after Henry IV's time. When the clock strikes three in *Julius Caesar*, we smugly remind Cassius that striking clocks were not invented until fourteen centuries after the death of Caesar. One of the minor pleasures of reading medieval romances is spotting the anachronism.

Setting an event, scene, person, or word in the wrong period is sometimes a slip, as I guess the cannon are in *King John*. Sometimes it is a deliberate literary device to distance events, and to underline a universal verisimilitude and timelessness, as I guess the reference to billiards in *Antony and Cleopatra* is. Shakespeare was a joker, as well as a genius, as well as a splendid hack who scribbled at great speed without always bothering to check facts and dates. 'Pedantry is only the scholarship of *le cuistre*. (We have no English equivalent)', wrote Walter Pater, unconsciously illustrating his point.
18

When Shaw referred to the Emperor as 'The Defender of the Faith' in *Androcles and the Lion*, I think he was just making a joke. But he used anachronism systematically and very effectively in *Saint Joan*. Much science fiction uses anachronism as a literary device. Dante used it to majestic effect in *The Divine Comedy*.

One of the most enjoyable anachronisms I know is in the Royal Museum of Fine Arts in Brussels. Among the glories of Flemish art hangs a large, stirring painting of the sack of Troy by one Peter Schoubroeck (1570–1607). In the background stands the ominous horse. The towers of Ilium are roasted in wrath and fire. There stands Hecuba, the 'mobbled' queen, i.e., with her face muffled. And in the foreground, for anybody who has not yet got the theme of the picture, stands a ruinous stone inscribed 'S.P.Q.T.' (*Senatus Populusque Troianus*), implying that the Trojans had a Senate and spoke Latin. I know that the Belgians are fond of inscribing 'S.P.Q.B.' on any official building or public monument; but this is ridiculous.

Anachronism is fun and an act of historical imagination, as well as a solecism to dull pedants. Strictly speaking, and we had better speak strictly on such a subject, anachronism puts something at a date that is too early, like Schoubroeck's Troy or Cassius counting the clock strike three; whereas parachronism puts something at a date that is too late, like making Aeneas meet Dido. Think how much in literature, music, and painting we should have missed, if Virgil had been careful about his dates.

Anachorism is the error of putting an action, scene, or character in a place where it does not belong. The most famous and engaging example is the stage direction in *The Winter's Tale*: 'Bohemia. A desert Country near the Sea.' Exit, pursued by a bare knowledge of geography.

Anachronism is getting your time out of joint. Anachorism is putting Bohemia by the sea. I have coined the word anatopism for getting your mountains topsy-turvy. A former managing director of mine, who has moved on to higher things, if such a concept is possible, recently turned up an interesting anatopism. He was giving a talk on the intellectual channel of the BBC, and employed the phrase 'Pelion upon Ossa'. He is a cultivated man, but his specialities are medieval French and works of reference, and his classics are rusty. A muttering arose from listening anatopism-spotters, who pointed out gleefully that Brewer, Lemprière, and other authorities had it vice versa, with the Giants piling Ossa upon Pelion in order to make their scaling-ladder to get at the Gods. Which is right?

Let us go back to the original sources. Homer, the originator of the catch-phrase, has the Giants setting out to pile Ossa on Olympus, and Pelion, with its shaggy forests, on top of Ossa, so that Heaven might be scaled. He further reports that they would have made this mountainous ladder, had they reached manhood; but Apollo slew them while they were still beardless boys.

So in Homer the planned piling order was Olympus at the bottom, Ossa in the middle, and Pelion on the top. A pedant might ask what on earth the Giants were up to, putting Olympus at the bottom; since Olympus was where the Gods lived, and where they were trying to get to.

It was Virgil who reversed the order of the mountains, and committed anatopism. In the *Georgics* he has, with marvellous, heaving spondees, the Giants three times trying to pile Ossa upon Pelion:

> 'Thrice they endeavoured—think of it—to heave
> Mount Ossa on Mount Pelion, and then roll,
> Forests and all, Olympus onto Ossa.
> Thrice with his bolt the Father razed that pile.'

I am sorry to have to tell you that he seems to have done this merely to suit the prosody of his hexameters, which seems to me a deplorably frivolous attitude to an important anatopism.

Homer was nearer to the source, and therefore a more reliable witness. On the other hand, for all I know, Homer set the piling order to suit his metre in the first place. The Giants were in no position to correct him. Probably the safest course is the cowardly one, adopted by Dryden, of avoiding naming names:

> 'With Mountains pil'd on Mountains, thrice they strove
> To scale the steepy Battlements of Jove.'

Anatopism, like anachronism, may prick pedants. Poets ignore it with impunity.

3/ BACK-MARKER

Mind your backs, please

> We all have something to fall back on, and I never knew a phony who didn't
> land on it eventually.
> Wilson Mizner (1876–1933)

Something a bit hearty in this chapter, chaps and chapesses. Hedge-row and humble tamarisk do not appeal to us all. If we must sing of athletics, let them be such as may do a ten-second hundred-metre sprinter honour.

Have you noticed what has been happening to *back-markers*? The *back-marker* used to be the fastest runner in a handicap race. He started from scratch, and had to overtake all the other runners, who started in front of him, in order to win the race. 'How brave a prospect is a bright backside!' wrote Henry Vaughan; though, I dare say, alas, that the mild poet was thinking of his beloved vanished county of Brecknock, rather than the *back-marker* in a handicap, straining on his marks on scratch. At any rate, it was too much for the Reverend H. F. Lyte, who amended the last two words to 'traversed plain' in his edition of Vaughan.

The final event of sports day, at some small English preparatory schools, anyway, used to be the school 440-yards handicap. The champion sprinter and head boy *ex officio* started from scratch and ran the full distance. The rest of the school were arranged in decreasing order of celerity nearer to the finishing tape, until the smallest boys had to toddle barely 100 yards. It was always popular with the impressionable mums if a villainous five-year-old pulled out a burst of speed he had not shown all season, and delighted the bookies by winning in a canter. It was usually arranged that this should happen.

21

The concept of *back-marker* was transferred to other sports and games where there was no literal scratch in the running-track for him to start behind. Here is an instance of this transferred use from the *Westminster Gazette* of 1899: 'One day there was an exhibition game of billiards. Captain Johnson took 150 in 300 from Cook, and had been passed by the *back-marker*.' That Captain Johnson sounds a regular snooker or rabbit at the old cannon-and-miscue nonsense.

In the last few years handicap racing has gone out of fashion. They still run it at the *Powderhall* in Edinburgh. The Stawell Gift Handicap is still the major contest in Australian professional athletics. But in most other races, except on sports day at small English prep schools, all runners start together from scratch. The *back-marker*'s occupation's gone from the running-track and the lexicon.

Accordingly commentators on horse, motor-car, motor-cycle, and human track racing have picked up the obsolete term, *back-marker*, and given it a new meaning. The usage has been affected by the modern automobile and motor-cycle starting grid. In these noisy and vile contests all the competitors cannot start together on scratch, or they would kill even more of each other than they do already. Accordingly, in order to avoid the risk of accidents and the perilous business of overtaking, those with the fastest lap-times in practice start at the front of the grid ahead of the rest of the field. Slowcoaches start from scratch. This is the opposite of the old handicap race, where the fastest started from scratch, and the slowest were given a handicap, in order, if the handicapper got the form right, that everybody should cross the finishing line simultaneously. Motor racing would be more 'exciting' and more lethal if it used the old-fashioned sort of *back-marker*.

For the front-marker in a Grand Prix race the advantage of the length of the starting-grid is minimal: perhaps two seconds in a two-hour race. However, the tactical benefits of getting one's bright back-side, decorated with tobacco advertisements, in front at the beginning may be considerable. In the old-fashioned handicap the slow runners might have had 100 or even 200 yards' start in a mile. Old-fashioned handicaps could be interesting Achilles-and-Tortoise affairs. Modern motor-racing is deeply boring because Achilles starts in front, and there is seldom much prospect of the Tortoise catching him up. The drivers at the back of the modern starting grid look like *back-markers* on scratch. But, instead of gradually overtaking the rest of the field, they (or their machines) are expected to perform least well. The meaning of *back-marker* has been turned arsy-versy over the past few years. From being the fastest runner in a race, the poor old *back-marker* has become the slowest.

Like *back-marker*, *tailback* is another sporting back that has recently changed its meaning. Stuck latish on a Sunday night in an apparently interminable traffic jam where the M1 meets the M6, and both are being constantly excavated, I thought of Mother Shipton. *The Prophecies of Mother Shipton*, ascribed to a mysterious lady of that name of 1641, or, by other accounts, of 1448, include the doggerel couplet:

> 'Carriage without horses shall go,
> And accidents fill the world with woe.'

Too right, Mother Shipton, I thought, as ten solid miles of motorists honked their horns, frayed their nerves, and shouted at their spouses. Roll on the day when the oil runs out, and we can go back to carriages with horses.

Ma Shipton was, alas, a forgery. Her disconcertingly accurate predictions were concocted by a London bookseller called Charles Hindley in 1862.

At this point the cheerful idiot on the radio caught up with our traffic jam, and started gloating about a *tailback* stretching from the Watford Gap to Spaghetti Junction. So I started thinking about the word *tailback*, which has arrived from the United States into the jargon of traffic-jam broadcasters. The image of a long, evil-smelling thing stretching for miles behind one is vivid. But the word *tailback* was originally used for a player in that silliest but most spectacular (in bursts of about two minutes in every hour) team game, American football.

In certain offensive formations the *tailback* is the back farthest from the line of scrimmage: he would be called the full back in rugby football. Specifically the basic I-formation has two backs lined up directly behind the quarter-back, the end is split, and one back plays wide as receiver. A variation of this is known as the power I: in this a fourth back is a running back at the side of the *tailback*.

I can see that all this is tedious gibberish to those of us who took our football in the Shed at Stamford Bridge or on the Mound at Twickenham, before the Rugby Football Union in its infinite wisdom replaced the Mound with stands. But in practice it can be quite exciting. You remember. Vast men in armour, like medieval knights, go into a huddle. Centre gives the 'snap', backward pass between his legs, to the quarter-back. Vast men charge and grapple like the first shock in the Battle of San Romano. Quarter-back hands off ball to half-back, who runs backwards at remarkable speed, and then, at the last moment, just before the chargers fall upon him, he rifles a long pass fifty yards to, say, a wide receiver, who will be running fast and well upfield. He will be the *tailback*, who has eluded the chargers, and has got to the front of the traffic jam. When it works, it is a beautiful spectacle. I just wish that the new *tailback* on motorways could elude the opposition and work his way to the front of the queue as quickly as he does in American footer, or as fast as the *back-marker* used to in handicap races.

4/ BEGGING THE QUESTION

Ideas that beggar description

> Asking for the thing in the beginning, or begging the question, is trying to show
> through itself something that is not knowable through itself.
> Aristotle, *Prior Analytics*, B16

We are uneasy about begging in our uneasy egalitarian age. I cannot
dig: to beg I am ashamed; which is the classic example of chiasmus,
or the criss-cross arrangement of parallel phrases for rhetorical effect.
He came out, and in went she. A superman in physique, but in intellect
a fool. *Omnis opera atque quaestus frequentia civium sustentatur,
alitur otio*: Cicero, *Against Lucius Sergius Catilina*, 4, 17: every
undertaking and enterprise is supported by the numbers of citizens,
by their leisure is nourished. It sounds like an attack on the British
Social Democratic Party for being the refuge of idle middle-class
dilettanti with no proper jobs to do. It is, however, a classic classical
example of chiasmus: the order of words in the first clause is inverted
in the second.

Begging leave and begging permission are stuffy, and obsolescent
commercialese. I suppose that there are still old-fashioned firms that
write 'I beg to advise you', and 'I beg to remain, Yours Faithfully.'
Beggar them. One could say, 'I beg your pardon', but it would mark
one as venerable as surely as a bowler hat or a rolled *Daily Telegraph*.

There have recently been a number of examples that indicate that
we misapprehend what it means 'to beg the question.' For instance,
an editorial in a trade paper the other day launched into its peroration
with: 'The question that now begs to be asked, however, is ...' This
managed to appear archaic, a Gallicism (by analogy with 'gives one
furiously to think'), and a misunderstanding of what it means to
beg the question.

25

To beg the question is not to ask it in a servile or old-fashioned way. It is to commit a fundamental error or side-step of logic by assuming the question under examination as proved, by founding a conclusion on a premise that needs to be proved as much as the conclusion itself. The 'argument' that 'fox-hunting is not cruel because the fox enjoys being hunted' begs the question. To state that parallel lines will never meet because they are parallel is to assume as a fact what one is professing to prove.

The formal Latin name in logic and rhetoric for begging the question is *petitio principii*. One common form of it is arguing in a circle, that is, the basing of two conclusions upon each other. The world must be good follows from the known goodness of God: God must be good because of the known excellence of the world he has made.

Other classic (though not circular) examples of begging the question are that capital punishment is necessary, because without it murders would increase; and that democracy must be the best form of government, because the majority must always be right. It may well be that the argument that high unemployment is inevitable in order to bring down inflation tends towards begging the question. But then, the dismal pseudo-science of economics sometimes seems nothing more than an elaborate system of begging the question.

Begging the question first appears in the arguing trades in Aristotle's *Topics*, where it means breaking the rules of the Academic game of elenchus. This is a game for two persons, the answerer and the questioner. The answerer asserts a thesis. The questioner then tries to refute him out of his own mouth, by asking him questions, and using his answers to contradict his original thesis.

For example, the answerer might assert as his thesis that philosophy is useless. The questioner might ask him whether philosophy is rational or irrational. If the answerer replied that philosophy is rational, the questioner would ask him whether rationality is useful or useless. If the answerer replied that it was useful, the questioner might say: 'Come now, let us put our admissions together. We have said that rationality is useful, and that philosophy is rational. It follows, therefore, contrary to your thesis, that philosophy is useful. I win a bottle of beer and a big kiss.'

Elenchus is a simple game, less exciting than space-invaders. I dare say that it could become boring. One of the rules of the game was that the questioner was not allowed to ask directly for his

26

conclusion. He might not directly put the question, 'Is philosophy useful?' Nor might he put the question indirectly by circumlocution, as, 'Does the study of the meaning of things and the truth benefit mankind?' Aristotle called this form of cheating, 'Asking for the beginning', which is badly translated into archaic English as begging the question. The Latin *petitio principii* is a less misleading translation.

The rule in the game, elenchus, has become an odd sort of logical fallacy. The two usual ways of destroying an argument are: first, to say that the conclusion does not follow from the premises; and second, to say that the premises are untrue. *Petitio principii* uses an unproved premise and an unproved conclusion tautologously to support each other, like two drunks leaning against each other to stop themselves falling over. It is an agreeable peculiarity that a rule of a game that nobody plays any more has become a misleadingly translated term for a common form of bogus reasoning.

While we are on about questions of rhetoric, let us put on the record for those being interviewed on television that a leading question is not a hostile one that goes to the nub and puts one on the spot. Person being interviewed, archly or angrily: 'Ahh, that's a leading question', implying: 'You are trying to lead me up the garden path, but I am too fly for your nasty tricks; pull the other one, it's got bells on.'

Au contraire, a leading question is not hostile, but friendly. It is one that suggests the proper or expected answer, especially in the law courts a question that leads a witness towards the answer that his lawyer would like him to make. It leads one not up the garden path, but in the back door; and judges consider it unfair. In English law some leading questions asked during examination-in-chief are considered inadmissible. Leading questions are permissible during cross-examination.

What has happened is a good example of the way the language grows. The established term, a leading question, is in the process of acquiring a secondary meaning. There is more amateur and fatuous questioning around than ever before in the history of human hot air, because of the recent great growth of broadcasting. Those being questioned need a term to describe the kind of question that the person being questioned feels is too probing and threatening. The language possesses no term for this, so the victim uses a term that sounds as though it answers the purpose. The awkward question is felt to be 'leading' because it penetrates the reserves and defences of the person being questioned. Occasions of confusion between the new popular meaning and the original lawyers' meaning will be few.

Our modern manual of rhetorical misapprehensions might usefully also notice the harmful use of the fanatic word 'demand' in wage and other industrial and political negotiations. There was a time when things were wanted and asked for; and frequently obtained, in spite of the mildness of the rhetoric. Some of our present industrial difficulties may be caused by reaction to the inflexible Ironside undertones in that Oliver Cromwell word, 'demand'. Maybe we should start to teach rhetoric in our schools again, at any rate as an optional extra, instead of social studies.

5/ BIKE

How another insult pedalled into the language

> Last night Cocklecarrot exclaimed, with his customary lucidity, that if a cow
> with handlebars is a bicycle, within the meaning of the Act, then a bicycle with
> four legs instead of two wheels is a cow.
> J. B. Morton (Beachcomber)

'On your bike, Shirl', I heard the pack of demonstrators shouting at
Mrs Shirley Williams, one of the leaders of the new British party of
Social Democrats. It was not a friendly shout; more of an insult. They
did not have in mind the observation of that Socialist Senor José
Antonio Viera Gallo, the Under-Secretary of Justice in the Chilean
Government of President Salvador Allende: *El socialismo puede
llegar solo en bicicleta* (Socialism can arrive only by bicycle).

'On your bike, Khomeini', the crowd shouted outside the Iranian
Embassy in London, while gunmen, shortly to be zapped by the SAS,
held hostages inside. It is an agreeably surreal image. But how could
one explain to the old monster the insult behind the literal meaning?

'On your bike', as an abusive instruction to push off and get lost,
has arrived in the repertoire of insult since about 1960, according to
Eric Partridge, that nice collector of such curiosities. It carries the
intimation that it will be the better for you if you get on your bike
promptly and pedal fast. There is some evidence that it may have been
around a bit longer than that, since the last war. It sounds like an
allied catchphrase to 'Mind my blue-pencil bike' from Jack Warner
(Dixon of Dock Green) in his early career as a World War Two
comic, featured as a strip cartoon in *Film Fun* in the 1940s.

The idiom is not confined to English. Americans say: 'Take a bike.'
The French say: *'Il a perdu ses pédales'*, indicating neatly and rudely
that the subject is no longer metaphorically in control of his bike. On

29

the morning after the unveiling of the large statue of Lenin in Krakow in 1970, commemorating the centenary of his birth, a bicycle was found hanging around its neck, with a message in Polish that he might find it useful for a return journey to Moscow. I do not know what to make of the Sikh student I saw on the campus of Delhi University wearing a T-shirt with the strange device: 'A man without a woman is like a fish without a bicycle.' No comment to that. But 'on your bike' is an apt new insult, since for some years the bicycle has been the fastest way of getting around the traffic-jammed cities of Europe and the United States.

The introduction of the push-bike as an insult into English breaks the normal pattern of swearing. Usually in the past insults have shocked by mentioning the unmentionable. So, in the ages of religion, the strongest oaths were derived from the deity, from blood and bloody to the more elaborately particular invocations of such awesome particles as God's toenail.

Now that God, sex, and excrement no longer shock most of us, it had been supposed that obscenity would attach to the last great unmentionable, death, and that insults would deal in coronaries and cancer. By the end of the century, it was said, the rudest insult available, after some cowboy had scraped your car, would be to leap out at the traffic-lights shouting: 'Are you blind, you putrefying old corpse?' How wrong we were! Bikes are rude. We shall be shouting: 'On your bike.'

After Cockneys, Australians are the most creative manufacturers of slang in English. It may have something to do with their convict and working class origins. The downtrodden are the best inventors of slang, because they get their own back on oppression and the harshness of life by shouting colourful insults at them. Oz already has its bike slang with different meanings. To get off one's bike means to lose one's temper.

For example, from Xavier Herbert's *Capricornia*, published in 1938: 'I tell you I saw no one!' 'Don't get off your bike, son. I know you're telling lies.'

For another example, from *The One Day of the Year* by Alan Seymour, 1962: Alf (yelling from kitchen), 'Where the bloody hell are you?' Mum (yelling back) 'Awright, don't get orf yr bike.'

The conciliatory phrase, 'I'll pick up your pump', used commonly to be appended to the injunction, 'Don't get off your bike.' The full statement indicates, with some nicety, that the speaker, although aware that the person he is addressing is in danger of losing his
30

temper, is prepared to appease him. It is a pity that the full statement is now little used, as it represents an economical statement of a conciliatory attitude, rather than the provocation offered in the truncated version. A crushing Liverpudlian variant, now obsolescent, was 'Awright, but don't get out of your pram.'

Also in Australian slang a bike is a promiscuous woman, usually in such expressions as 'the town bike' and 'the office bike'. It is derived from the use of 'ride' for the male role in intercourse. For example, from *Jimmy Brockett* by Dal Stivens, 1951: 'I might have known you were the bloody town bike.' And, more recently, from David Williamson's *The Removalists*, 1972: 'Turned out the tart was the biggest bike in the district.' As Dale Spender has remarked, it is a sign of the masculine bias of English, particularly Australian English, that there are so many words for a promiscuous woman, and so few, generally jocular, for a promiscuous man.

Partridge, in his *Dictionary of Slang and Unconventional English*, suggested that this use of bike as an insult for a loose woman, because she is so often and generally ridden, was Australian from circa 1920. I have received a considerable correspondence from places as far apart as Aberdeenshire and Shropshire, claiming that the metaphor is not Australian but Aberdonian, or, as it might be, Salopian. A High Court judge wrote to say that in 1930, in a Gloucestershire Magistrates' Court, he heard a young man give evidence in a bastardy case. He said of the girl complainant: 'She was the village bike.' 'What do you mean by that?' asked the Chairman. 'Everybody rode her,' was the reply. The idiom is evidently widely diffused, and there is little profit in trying to establish who invented it.

Less widely diffused is the Australian insult that eluded Partridge's collections of slang and catch phrases: 'You play cricket with me, Jack, and I'll shove the bat up your arse.' I get the general drift, but I do not see it catching on in Aberdeenshire.

Leonardo da Vinci is supposed to have designed the first machine driven by cranks and pedals with connecting rods. The precursor of the modern bicycle was the *célérifère* or *vélocifère*, built for the Comte de Sivrac, and demonstrated at the Palais Royal in Paris in 1791. It was a sort of wooden horse on two wheels, propelled by a rider sitting astride, who pushed the apparatus along with alternate thrusts of his feet. We have pedalled a long way since then, on the road and in the vocabulary of insult.

6/ CATCH-22

There is no such thing as a simple catch

A fronte praecipitium, a tergo lupus.
Latin proverb: In front a precipice, behind a wolf; or, just about, out of the frying-pan into the fire

It is easier for a camel to pass through the knee of an idol than for a catch-phrase to pass into the English language with its precise meaning unimpaired. *Catch-22* is a fashionable catch-phrase of political and media rhetoric that is widely and inaccurately used. Because it is such a pretty, knowing phrase, it is now used to describe any awkward situation, rather than a hidden dilemma based on a puzzling paradox.

Catch-22 is the title of a very funny, angry novel by the American Joseph Heller, published in 1961. The title refers to a paradoxical and fictional rule of the United States Air Force in the last war: a pilot must carry on flying combat missions until he is judged insane or otherwise unfit; if he carries on flying into the anti-aircraft fire without asking to be relieved, he is probably insane; if, however, he formally asks to be relieved, he is adjudged sane, and may not be relieved. Either way, sane or insane, you keep on flying until you are finally given your wings by the Great Pilot in the Sky.

This marvellously zany concept has become popular in journalese. International conferences are said to suffer from a universal *Catch-22*, which states that any problem we can solve is part of a larger problem that we cannot solve. Because discrimination prevented women, black, and other minority workers from getting jobs in the past, they have no seniority; because they have no seniority, they are the first to be laid off in a recession. That is a loose sort of *Catch-22*. You cannot have a job unless you have a

32

union card, and you cannot have a union card unless you have a job. That was the old trade union joke (?), years before Heller wrote, but a true *Catch-22*. You can't get on Broadway without Broadway experience. With unemployment at its high level, many young people are discovering that one cannot gain experience without a job, but one cannot get a job without experience. Both genuine *Catch-22s*. Sequels to films are said to suffer from a *Catch-22*: in order to sell, stress has to be laid on the original success; but, the more sharply focused these memories of the earlier hit, the more pallid the sequel seems. *Jaws 2*, about a woman-eating shark, was cited as a *Catch-22* in point.

A cruel form of Soviet *Catch-22*, used against dissidents or those who wish to emigrate, is to dismiss them from their jobs, make it impossible for them to get work of any kind, and then prosecute them for not working. The classic forefather of the *Catch-22* was the *Hauptmann von Koepenick*, a play by Carl Zuckmayer. It is based on real events in the Kaiser's Germany. Cobbler, released from prison, decides to go straight, goes to police station, and asks for a *Arbeitsbuch* or work permit. Police tell him that he will be given a work-book once he has found employment, but that no employer will offer him a job until he has handed over his work-book. There is your true, your blushful *Catch-22*. Cobbler dresses up as Captain in the Imperial Guards, orders the Burgomaster of Koepenick, a small town near Berlin, to hand over the work-book to the cobbler, changes back into his old clothes, and all seems well. However, news of the hoax gets out, I am afraid, and the cobbler ends up in his old *Catch-22* and jail again. It is a simple story, but, at the time, it was a popular satirical attack on German nomomania and deference to Prussian authority.

Catch-22 permits the enforcement of a rule nullifying a right, the exercise of which gives rise to the rule. Put less formally, *Catch-22* exists where the only way out of a sticky situation leads you straight back into the molasses. Occasions are rare in which such a pretty notion can be applied precisely. Nevertheless, it is a pity that it is being blunted by loose use to mean any old difficulty, with no element of paradox.

The hyperbolical Americans have now introduced a Catch-23, intended to be an even stickier minestrone to fall into than a *Catch-22*. There is said to be a Catch-23 in the global oil business. Put simply, the idea is that to escape the political clutches of OPEC and any other *cartel*, the West will have to develop vast new sources

33

of energy. The Catch-23 is that the very act of producing all this new energy may lead to a glut of oil and a sharp drop in its price, thus undercutting the price of the new energy. Generalizing, if we want to make Catch-23 formal, and I am not sure that we do apart from a clever journalistic phrase, we could say that Catch-23 exists where the only practicable remedy for a situation has the effect of rendering that remedy impracticable. In fact the Catch-23 formula seems merely a restatement in obtuse form of the familiar economic principle that, if you generate supply to an extent that exceeds demand, prices will fall. If the new sources of energy were in fact oil, precisely the same results would follow.

Double-bind is an even newer vogue phrase that is widely used by journalists for an awkward and paradoxical situation, something like a *Catch-22*. Like *Catch-22* it originally had a sharp meaning that has been blunted by misunderstanding. *Double-bind* was invented as a precise term of anthropology and psychology. It was developed by the anthropologist, Gregory Bateson, to describe the situation in which expectation is continually frustrated, as when a child, for example, is given rules to obey which conflict, and yet cannot be ignored. In Bali, Bateson found that such an upbringing produced a balanced and temperate adult. In other cultures it was found to contribute either to schizophrenia or to the development of 'trans-contextual' creative abilities. As such, it was enthusiastically taken up by R. D. Laing and his disciples about fifteen years ago.

Serious troubles are said to arise when a mother's normal life becomes subject to promptings from her unconscious. The child of such a parent finds himself repeatedly caught in a *double-bind*, that is in a situation in which he is given simultaneous but mutually contradictory cues, so that whatever he does will be wrong.

We may well suspect that the assertions of psychology are un-proved and unprovable, and its jargon Psychobabble. We may well be uneasy that the social sciences generally turn over stones and show us things about ourselves underneath them that we find un-comfortable. But what is happening to *double-bind* and *Catch-22* is a common pattern of misappropriated technicalities. We journal-ists and other magpies of language and ideas hear a smart new piece of jargon. We like its glitter and the air of learning it conveys. The didactic urge is strong; so is the urge to show off. So we pick it up, without troubling to find out exactly what it means, and use it to decorate our discourse. That is a way the language changes.

7/ COHORT

To the legion of the lost ones, to the cohort of the damned

The Assyrian came down like the wolf on the fold,
And his cohorts were gleaming in purple and gold.
Byron, *Destruction of Sennacherib*

I am the mildest of editors, taking up the red biro with distaste.
If somebody is good enough to review a book in *The Times*, he
or she is good enough to have the review printed as written, without
tinkering. Otherwise, it might as well be done again. Michael Frayn's
definition of sub-editing was for *The Guardian*, not *The Times*:
'Nothing to it, old boy; check all facts and spellings; cut the first
and last sentences; and remove all attempts at jokes.'

But I did a ruthless piece of subbing a while ago, and on a piece
from a Professor of English Literature. He had written *cohort* in
a context that made it clear that what he had in mind was a comrade
or associate. This recent change in the semantics of *cohort* is
recognized by the newest dictionaries, such as *The Oxford American
Dictionary* published in 1981, which gives for the second meaning,
'an associate, an accomplice.'

It grates on the ears of Latinists, who remember that a *cohort*
was originally not a single companion, but a battalion of infantry.
The Romans had *cohorts* of *socii* that were five hundred strong
(*cohortes quingenariae*), or a thousand strong (*cohortes milliariae*).
They even had a *cohors amicorum*, which was the entourage of friends
and acquaintances on the make that a provincial governor or an
emperor took around with him wherever he went.

Now it is true that we can no longer run the English language
so as to avoid wounding the susceptibilities of classical scholars.
We never have been able to. The new, unclassical use of 'decimate',

35

meaning to wipe out almost everybody present by slaughter or disease, has prevailed. Why, even Charlotte Brontë used it loosely: 'Typhus fever decimated the school.' And here is De Tocqueville in *La Démocratie en Amérique*, published 1835–40: '*Les croisades et les guerres des Anglais déciment les nobles et divisent leurs terres.*' And the old Roman use of decimate to mean to execute one in ten of mutinous, insubordinate, cowardly, or merely unsuccessful soldiers in a *cohort*, to encourage the others, is no longer a very useful word. In the Roman Republic decimation was one of the main reasons why the *cohorts* tended to carry on fighting, while their enemies' virtue ran away to their legs.

Opportunities to use the word 'decimate' are rare these days, outside the study of ancient history; and it is no great loss that 'decimate' is widely used to mean to destroy a large part of. For anyone who remembers any Latin at all, 'decimate' wears the sense of tenth or tithe as plainly as the *cohorts* wore their helmets. It causes such a person grief and vexation to use the word innumerately as well as illiterately, as in, 'they decimated nearly half the enemy', or, 'the fire decimated nine-tenths of the town.' Such persons are going to have to swallow their vexation and grief. The new meaning has come to stay. It is not yet compulsory for those of us who dislike it to use it in its expanded, imprecise sense.

But what are we to do about this strange new *cohort*, in the singular meaning of companion or mucker? We can guess that the new vogue use of *cohort* satisfies some need in the lexicon. We can resolve not to use it in that way ourselves until at least it is more firmly established. We can note with gratification that biologists have adapted the word more sensibly than the rest of us for their specialized jargon, when they use *cohort* as a taxonomic group that is a subdivision of a subclass (usually of mammals) or subfamily (of plants). The word is quite suitably applied to plants, since its Latin etymology is connected with *hortus*, a garden. And we can speculate about how the change in *cohort* has happened, because such speculation may be instructive about the way language changes generally.

One line of approach is to suppose that there has been confusion between *cohort* and the American colloquial word *cahoot*, a company or partnership, as in 'in cahoots with.' The *OED* derives 'cahoot' from the French *cahute*, a hut, cabin, or shanty. But some American dictionaries refer it to the French *cohorte*. The *OED* gives sense 3 of *cohort* as, 'A company, band; especially of persons united in

36

defence of a common cause; a figurative meaning.' It seems that there is a certain amount of common ground here that might give rise to the use of *cohort* with the meaning of working together, and so a companion. Another way of putting that last sentence would be to say that the *Oxford English Dictionary* and the *Oxford American Dictionary* are going round in circles, and slipshod usage is following them.

Another line of march to the new *cohort* lies through more extravagant terrain. Before you dismiss it as frivolous, remember that Fowler himself, in desperation, wondered whether the strange and anomalous usage of 'or otherwise' might derive from a feeble joke. 'No organizations, religious or otherwise, have troubled to take the matter up.' What can have possessed anybody in such a context to write 'otherwise' instead of 'other'? Is it not (far-fetched and frivolous as the explanation may seem) that the old saying 'Some men are wise and some are otherwise' once struck the popular consciousness as witty, and has incidentally inspired a belief that 'otherwise', and not 'other', is the natural parallel to an adjective?

Here is a far-fetched explanation of the strange new *cohorts* we meet with increasing frequency. I find it persuasive.

The use of *cohort* to mean associate, or accomplice, comes from the United States. In America Byron has a greater reputation than here: in fact, as high as his continental reputation. A favoured poem is the one about Sennacherib, the wolf-on-the-fold chappie, as Bertie Wooster would say, whose *cohorts*, in the second line, were said to be gleaming with purple and gold. Imagine a scene in some Little Red Schoolhouse in the Mid-West. Little Abe asks: 'What are *cohorts*, Miss?' Miss, with her attention fixed on the central figure of Sennacherib rather than the Assyrian troops, replies, 'His courtiers', (or 'his attendants'). I think that this famous poem may well be the source of the new sense of *cohort*, because the people who brought the new usage into fashion are not likely to have been students of the Roman army. The explanation has an eccentricity that is irresistible.

8/ DISBENEFIT

Time to suspend our disbelief in Jungle English?

Let him who bestows the benefit conceal it, let him who receives it reveal it.
Seneca, *De Beneficiis*, II, c. 63

A new word is being hatched into the vast flock of the English lexicon. The word is *disbenefit*. There have been several sightings of it in Officialese dealing with social security matters, but none so clear as to make plain exactly what it means. The word is too new to have been included in the first volume of the *OED Supplement*, published in 1972. It did not make *Collins* (1979) or *Longman* (1982). It must, I guess, mean more than a simple disadvantage like having one's house in the middle of the proposed Number One runway of London's third airport, or in the centre of a dense pack of MX missiles, grouped so that incoming Soviet missiles would destroy each other by fratricide while trying to destroy them.

Perhaps *disbenefit* means something intended to be a benefit which in practice is not: for example, the agreeable reduction in bus and Underground fares, paid for out of the rates, for somebody living in a highly rated London Borough who never travels by public transport. It might have something to do with the poverty trap, a flaw at the bottom end of the British taxation system, by which something intended to make one better off in hard buff-coloured fact has the opposite effect.

As often happens, the recent vague and vogue extension of the word grew out of a muddily apprehended piece of specialized jargon. *Disbenefit* started life, in the admittedly specialized and hermetic world of British public-sector investment project appraisal (you can note with a sharp intake of breath the sort of jargon those gnomes of public-sector Whitehall use), to mean the opposite of a benefit.

It was used in the report of the Roskill Commission into the Third London Airport published in 1971, and I suspect its use goes back a few years before that.

Let us take this slowly. In a cost-benefit analysis one may find that while some of the effects of the project in question are beneficial, others are deleterious, and should therefore be counted on the other side of the balance sheet. Noise nuisance was the main *disbenefit* identified in the Roskill report. If it is assumed that adequate compensation for the nuisance will be paid by the sponsor of the project, then the *disbenefit* becomes a cost, no different in principle from the construction or operating costs. However, it is not always, or even often, the case that the sponsor pays compensation for the *disbenefits* of his project. Accordingly, it is apparently useful to those who deal with such matters to have a word to describe the items on the cost side of the balance sheet that do not represent actual transfers of money.

(Exasperated and frivolous aside: benefits are still conferred by benefactors. Malefactors used to commit malefactions. Why could they not still be said to do so, rather than *disbenefits*, or, perhaps, stretching a point, commit malefits?)

Disbenefit is, I suspect, related by analogy to a diseconomy. In the jargon of economics, a diseconomy means the opposite of an economy, specifically an increase in costs arising when a business exceeds an 'optimum size'. When a firm, or a school, or some other organization expands above a certain point, administrative costs, a lengthening of the management hierarchy, and the growth of bureaucracy and bumf produce diseconomies of scale, in increased costs per unit of output or child education. In newspaper offices such diseconomies tend to occur on what Antipodean slang describes engagingly as 'the mahogany floor', that is, the floor furnished with mahogany desks and non-writing executives, whose sole function sometimes seems, to their hard-pressed hacks, to be to impede those who actually produce the paper. In armies diseconomies of scale are indicated by the growth of tail, or support units, and the shrinkage of teeth, or fighting men.

Economists are the clodhoppers of language. Their jargon, *disbenefits*, diseconomies, and all, is the muddiest, even including that of sociologists and psychologists; and those are fighting words. The last economist to use English lucidly was John Stuart Mill. That may seem rather unfair on J. K. Galbraith; but, let it stand, let it stand.

39

What are we to make of *disbenefit*? The jolliest recent example was back on dear old London Transport in 1982. Workers on the Underground and buses get free tickets by virtue of their jobs. When the new Labour Greater London Council cut fares drastically, these workers were given gratuities to compensate for their *disbenefit*.

As long ago as 1935 A. P. Herbert, the wit and very independent Member of Parliament for Oxford University, was campaigning against the notion that one can take a good word, put a dis-, de-, re-, in-, un-, or non- in front of it, and come up with an equally good word. His APHorism was that nobody would think of saying non-sober when he meant drunk. A.P.H., up in his celestial book-room, must be fit to be tied to look down and see that any number of social scientists today not only think of it, but actually say non-sober, as a more impressive or less wounding way of saying drunk; just as they say developing to mean poor nations, and disadvantaged to mean poor people. Social scientists would reply firmly to the last point that they use 'disadvantaged' to mean more than the customary connotations of 'poor'.

A.P.H. particularly disliked 'disequilibrium', usually financial disequilibrium found in the financial pages of *The Times*. He fought a long, gallant, and losing campaign with the newspaper over it. He argued that equilibrium was an exact word—an absolute word, like 'absolute' or 'unique'. To prefix dis- to it did not make another exact word; it made a vague and feeble word. He liked disequilibrium as little as he would have liked disabsolutely for 'not quite', or disunique for 'common'. Why talk about disassembling an engine, as certain rude mechanicals in the motor trade do? The engineers of the Royal Navy say 'strip an engine'—short and sweet, metaphorical and true. Even the great and good A. P. Herbert was unable to think of an alternative way of describing 'a pact of non-aggression'.

Well, A.P.H. lost disequilibrium, just as he lost non-sober. Those monstrous jargonauts the economists have found a precise use for disequilibrium and diseconomy, which they say have meanings that cannot be expressed any other way without intolerable circumlocution, as if intolerable circumlocution were not the element in which they live, and move, and have their being.

It is their technical jargon, and we must leave them to get on with it. The rest of us can allow ourselves a bitter smile, as it becomes increasingly evident that, even if they understand their own jargon, in the real world they do not know their arses from their elbows.

40

'Deselection', as threatened to British Labour Members of Parliament who lose the confidence of their constituency party committees, is another new non-word. It means to take back the party's nomination from the peccant or unfortunate or unfashionable M.P. A.P.H. called such words 'jungle words'. Deselection sounds to me like a euphemism for the brutal truth of 'sack', 'get rid of', 'dismiss', 'give the old heave-ho'. It is just as well that the fanatics and barbarians have not yet thought of a 'deseating' or even a 'delifing' solution for their moderate comrades.

I am informed by a Ghanaian wordsmith that in Ghana 'destooling' is commonly used when an Akan chief is deprived of his authority. In the north of Ghana, where the skin is the symbol of chieftaincy, a deposed chief is said to be 'deskinned'. Surely the penalty for using all such jungle words should be debagging?

9/ FORENSIC

A funny thing happened on the way from the forum

The law is a sort of hocus-pocus science, that smiles in yer face while it picks yer pocket.
Charles Macklin, *Love à la Mode*, II, 1761

A society of men bred up from their youth in the art of proving by words multiplied for the purpose that white is black and black is white according as they are paid. Lawyers, I am afraid, M'lud; according to that satirical rogue, Jonathan Swift.

Swift was, at any rate, correct in saying that barristers make their living by the word. It is, accordingly, more deplorable, as well as more funny, when a piece of jargon of professional wordsmiths goes wrong, than when some civilian word used by ordinary men starts to go off the rails. The word I have in mind is *forensic*. The notion seems to be spreading that *forensic* means 'scientific', particularly scientific in an investigatory, Sherlock Holmesian way, messing about with bloodstains and footprints and little monographs on the ashes of one hundred and forty different varieties of pipe, cigar, and cigarette tobacco.

It means nothing of the sort, as any fool, even a lawyer, can see. The meaning of *forensic* stands out of the face of the word like a Roman nose. It comes directly from the Latin *forensis*, the adjective of *forum*, evolving in the same way that *castrensis* is the adjective of *castra*, a camp. The forum was the market-place and public square in Roman towns, the place of assembly. In Rome itself there was a series of *fora* or forums stretching from the early Republic to the late Empire, and from the Colosseum to the Piazza Venezia. The forum of a Roman town was the place for the transaction of judicial and other public business, for lawyers and politicians.

42

Forensic was brought into English to mean 'legal', pertaining to courts of law; and, for more than four centuries, until its sudden recent giddiness, it has carried its original, etymologically exact meaning, and minded its own business. Now it has become a vogue word. Every week I bump into an example of *forensic* examination, when there is no question of the result of the examination being used in a court of law or in any other legal form. I am continually stumbling over *forensic* evidence in court reports: a pleonasm, since any evidence given in court is, by definition, *forensic*.

I think that the shift began because of misapprehension of the persons described as *forensic* scientists or *forensic* experts. These specialists are likely to be given pieces of physical evidence from sensational criminal cases to examine, and then called to give evidence in court about the results of their investigations. In the United Kingdom Sir Bernard Spilsbury (1877–1947) was the great *forensic* pathologist, who gave evidence at nearly every murder trial in the south of England in the first half of this century. His methodical habits, phenomenal memory, and passion for detail influenced not merely *forensic* practice but a generation of detective fiction.

We have got hold of the wrong end of the stick, and suppose that *forensic* refers to the scientific rather than the legal performance of such fellows as Spilsbury. In fact our *forensic* experts are our judges and professors of law, persons not likely to be found sifting ashes or measuring footprints, and not likely to be very good at such activities if they tried.

Forensic is a choice new example of what Fowler termed a popularized technicality: a piece of precise technical jargon that was only partly understood by the general public, and adopted as a vague vogue word, to decorate their language with a spurious air of professional expertise. 'Acid test' was the most fashionable popularized technicality when Fowler was writing in the Twenties. Acid test has become old-fashioned in chemistry as a way of testing for gold by means of aquafortis, and old-fashioned in language as a metaphor for a crucial test.

But popularized technicalities are as popular as they ever were in careless talk; more popular, probably, since there are so many new branches of science producing so many new discoveries and so much new jargon. One of the most prolific and imprecise in our Age of Anxiety is the Psychobabble of Freudian English. The jargon of psychology is in any case a jungle, even when used by the professionals. The schools of Freud, Jung, Adler and the others often mean distinctly different things by the same technical word. It is no wonder that outsiders are confused about this fashionable vocabulary, and use 'schizophrenic' to mean undecided, 'obsessive' to mean punctual, 'psychopathic' to mean cruel, and 'trauma' to mean an upset or inconvenience. 'Mrs R., wife of a Texas business-man, a tall handsome woman, refused a glass of champagne. "It makes me sneeze", she said. "And I don't feel masochistic enough to drink champagne right now."'

Other examples of popular modern popularized technicalities are:

From medicine: clinical, test-tube (baby), syndrome.

From the prolific source of Computerese: interface, hardware and software and wetware.

From economics: monetarist, Keynesian.

From mathematics and statistics: proportion, differential, quantum leap, parameter; 'She and Harry hadn't finalized the parameters of their own interface.'

From lit. crit.: Catch-22, theatre of the absurd, elegiac, euphuism.

From chess: stalemate, gambit, checkmate.

From cricket: hat-trick, bodyline.

From theology and sociology: charisma, theology itself as a term of abuse intended to indicate something obscure and useless, like the Labour Party's Constitution.

From Defence jargon: low profile, escalate, unilateral.

From philosophy: dilemma, optimism and pessimism, philosophy itself, as in, 'the Company is planning to introduce a whole new marketing philosophy.'

From architecture: flamboyant, baroque, rococo, modernism.

That is a tiny, eclectic sample. With a systematic effort we could compile a whole book doing nothing but list popularized technicalities. It would be a dull read.

Fowler objected to popularized technicalities because they misrepresented, sometimes very badly, the original meanings of the technical jargon; and because free indulgence in them resulted in a tawdry style. These quasi-scientific clichés look impressive. Their use evokes and even releases emotion. They have the knowing look of key concepts of modern thought; and nobody is quite sure what they mean.

I am afraid that the general public pays not a blind bit of interest to the scruples of purists; even such spendid purists as the great and good Fowler. But the misapprehension of *forensic* and its fashionable new use do seem a wicked waste. We have 'scientific' to do the job that *forensic* has been shanghaied to mean; and nothing to replace the original meaning of *forensic* exactly in one word.

10/ FORMAT

Mr Pecksniff knew the format

> Language is purely a species of fashion, in which by the general, but tacit, consent of the people of a particular state or country, certain sounds come to be appropriated to certain things as their signs.
> George Campbell, *The Philosophy of Rhetoric*, 1776

Mr Pecksniff, we are told, was in the frequent habit of using any word that occurred to him as having a good sound, and rounding a sentence well, without much care for its meaning. It is a free country. People can use words to mean what they want, provided that they do not object to being misunderstood. Nevertheless, I wish that the innocent advertisers would stop making me giggle as I walk around London by plastering the walls with banners with the strange device: FAGGOTS—GREAT BALLS OF GOODNESS.

Format has recently been picked up as a vogue word, which has a good sound and rounds a sentence well, without much care for its meaning. It originally had a precise meaning in the publishing and bookish world: the shape and size of a book, for example quarto or octavo. Its root etymology is from the Latin *formatus* (sc. *liber*), and it came into English by way of French in the nineteenth century.

Suddenly, through love of the longer word and lust for elegant variation with an expert sound, we have started to use *format* as a synonym for 'form', 'layout', 'arrangement', 'design', or any old thingummyjig. A recent letter to *The Times* from the president of the Glasgow Bar Association exemplified the new *format*—sorry, the new misuse: 'Courts, at which—in present *format*—the solicitor has no right of audience.' In the same week the Diary of the same paper contained the sentence: 'The size of Hansard will change to A4, but the *format* will remain the same.' Since *format* means the

46

shape and size of a book, the juxtaposition of 'size' and *format* managed to be both incongruous and tautologous.

Chartered accountants now talk and write constantly of the *format* of their accounts. Here is a pretty plum from a trade newsletter: 'The Annual Ball has now added a tombola and a steel band to its attractions, thus departing from its traditional *format*.' And here is a notice from the club secretary on a club notice-board: 'The new bedrooms are nearly completed, but the *format* has not yet been decided. Suggestions from members will be welcomed.' I guess that the club secretary meant the decoration or furniture or arrangement of the bedrooms. 'Do you like your sheets folded quarto or octavo, Sir?' But, instead of making his meaning clear, he reached for the fashionable, new, all-purpose *format*. In most of the other examples 'form' would be clearer as well as shorter. Economy is a virtue in language as well as in shopping.

It is no good complaining that the new meaning is wrong or trying to ban it. Good men have been trying to purify English of such vogue misunderstandings for centuries. John Milton wrote that he supported 'him who endeavours by precept and by rules to perpetuate that style and idiom of speech and composition which have flourished in the purest periods of the language.' Dryden regretted that, 'speaking so noble a language as we do, we have not a more certain measure of it as they have in France, where they have an Academy enacted for that purpose and endowed with large privileges by the present king.' Edmund Bolton first proposed the *format* of an Academy for Pure English in 1617. Samuel Butler supported the scheme, as did Swift in the following century. He urged that *The Tatler* exercise its authority as censor, 'and by an annual *index expurgatorius* expunge all words and phrases that are offensive to good sense.' A year later, on 4 August 1711, *The Spectator* agreed with him.

There was a strong feeling, then as now, that English was being corrupted by two classes, the pedants and the trendy. Swift, in his *Proposals for Correcting the English Language*, complained of the young men who, 'terribly possessed with the fear of pedantry, run into a worse extreme ... borrowing the newest set of phrases, and if they take a pen into their hands, all the odd words they have picked up in a coffee-house, or a gaming ordinary, are produced as flowers of style.'

Swift went on, and he did go on: 'But what I have most at heart is that some method should be thought on for ascertaining and fixing

47

our language forever, after such alterations are made in it as shall be thought requisite.' In his *Plan* for his *Dictionary* Samuel Johnson wrote: 'One great end of this undertaking is to fix the English language.' But in the *Preface* to the published work (1755), he acknowledged the impossibility of such an undertaking: 'If the changes we fear be thus irresistible, what remains but to acquiesce with silence, as in the other insurmountable distresses of humanity? It remains that we retard what we cannot repel, that we palliate what we cannot cure. Life may be lengthened by care, though death cannot be ultimately defeated: tongues, like governments, have a natural tendency to degeneration; we have long preserved our constitution, let us make some struggles for our language.'

And so say all of us. But I doubt whether we can retard the advance of *format* to occupy new meanings. I think that the craze for *format* may have spread immediately from the jargon of television, where it is fashionable to talk of the *format* of a programme, when what is meant is its style, plan, or arrangement. When tempted to write *format*, resolve, Philip, to remember the moral Pecksniff, and write 'form'; in the same way remember to write 'exact' rather than 'meticulous', 'other' rather than 'alternative', 'total' rather than 'overall', and 'some' rather than 'a percentage'.

Shortly after I had discussed the shift in the meaning of *format*, I received a charming letter from a computer called Tom (whose name derives from Thoroughly Obedient Moron). Tom pointed out that *format* went from English first into Fortran, the computer-programming language developed in the fifties, and then back into English, which sort of legitimizes its descent. Tom works in a language that demands total clarity and precision. He is too stupid to ignore mistakes or worry out half-meanings. A *format* statement instructs the computer about the form data, numbers, and letters will take, as well as the arrangement and size of the page. Most technologists these days can write Fortran, yet their written English is remarkably undisciplined. Perhaps the intention is to flatter the reader that he is much cleverer than a computer.

Here is Tom's letter—

DEAR MR HOWARD
RE: 'FORMAT'
FORTRAN IS A COMPUTER PROGRAMMING LANGUAGE USED FOR TECHNICAL WORK. IN IT, 'FORMAT' IS AN INSTRUCTION TO ME TO SET OUT MY PRINTOUT

ACCORDING TO THE LAYOUT DEFINED WITHIN A PAIR
OF BRACKETS IMMEDIATELY AFTER 'FORMAT'.
AS A VERY SIMPLE EXAMPLE, SUPPOSE I HAVE ARRIVED
AT THREE NUMBERS CALLED A, B, AND C. IF YOU
INSTRUCT ME
FORMAT ('A =', F5.2,/, 'B =', F5.2,/,M 'C =', F5.2)
I WOULD GO ON STRIKE, BECAUSE THE LETTER 'M'
SHOULDN'T BE THERE, AND IT CONFUSES ME.
IF YOU ERASE THE 'M', THEN I WILL PRINT:

A = 34.56

B = 57.07

C = 4.23

IT'S ALL A BIT CUMBERSOME, BUT THEN I AM
EXTREMELY DIM, AND SO MY INSTRUCTIONS HAVE TO
BE VERY DETAILED AND ABSOLUTELY PRECISE.
YOURS SINCERELY
TOM

Computer technology is one of the most prolific and prolix new sources of jargon. It has given us new meanings for 'hardware', 'software', even 'wetware', which means, rather disgustingly, the human brain, 'real-time', and dozens of others. In Computerese *format* has a precise and useful meaning, as set out eloquently by my friend, Tom. In the real world, outside computers and publishing, 'form' is usually a better word.

11/ FRAUGHT

Fraught train of thought

Swell, bosom, with thy fraught,
For 'tis of aspics' tongues.
Shakespeare, *Othello*, III, 3, 447

I am *fraught* with intimations of impermanence about the word *fraught*. It is a fashionable word. Here are a couple of examples from fashionable journalists. 'In matters of Love the *fraught* old courtships of such partners as André [Previn] and Mia [Farrow] and even Roddy [Llewellyn] and Margaret [Princess—well, this was in a vulgar journal] have been overtaken by the new-style public pairing of Billy Connolly and Pamela Stephenson.' And another: 'The position of Labour's Right on the National Executive is also more *fraught* than the victory headlines suggested.'

I caught myself saying it the other day. Somebody telephoned for a general discussion of life and literature on a Tuesday afternoon while I was making up the Books Page. How were things, she asked at last, after telling me at length how things were with her. 'Pretty *fraught*', I heard myself replying, with a gusty sigh of resignation.

This is a recent shift of meaning; too recent to be recorded in any but the most recent dictionaries. In the six centuries of the word's history in English until the last few years, things or people had to be *fraught with* something, not *fraught* absolutely, on their own.

It was originally an Ancient Mariner's nautical word, meaning laden *with* something; thence it came to mean stored or supplied *with* something; and thence, transferred by metaphor, it came to mean attended *with* something. It came to us from the sea-faring and sea-trading Dutch, who had in Middle Dutch up until the fourteenth century the same word, *vrachten*. Etymologists detect
50

probable correspondence with the Old High German word *freht*, meaning earnings.

Here are some examples of the former literal and transferred uses of *fraught* from assorted masters of Eng. Lit. Macaulay: 'His painted bark of cane. *Fraught* for some proud bazaar's arcades ...' Bacon wrote of the works of Pliny being *fraught* with much fabulous matter. The fifteenth-century *Book of St Albans*: 'A shippe *fraught* full of hawkis.' Spenser: 'That all the world shold with his rimes be *fraught*.' Shelley: 'A loftier Argo cleaves the main, *Fraught* with a later prize.' Swift wrote majestically of a large memory, plentifully *fraught* with Theological Polysyllables.

Words do change their meanings to meet new needs; otherwise we should still be using 'crafty' to mean strong and 'silly' to mean defenceless. *Fraught* itself has gradually expanded its meaning over the past six centuries to include all sorts of loads as well as the kind carried in the holds of merchant ships. But when a British poet and novelist can write: 'Sleep didn't often withhold her favours from me, but if she did it was always when the next day was going to be particularly *fraught*,' the word has made a sudden jump in semantics to mean something like distressing (in other contexts, distressed). It has lost its original literal connexion with sea transport. And it is being used absolutely, not *fraught with* or full of anything, just *fraught*, *tout court*.

There is no point in crying 'Foul!', or complaining that this is not what *fraught* means, and that it is a solecism to use the past participle absolutely. There is some point in trying to understand how and why the shift in meaning has happened.

As soon as it left the docks, one of the early figurative meanings of *fraught* was big with promise or menace of something or other, which was always specified. The English, being people who expect the worst and are seldom disappointed, tended to be *fraught* with the latter meaning of doom rather than the former meaning of promise. A sixteenth-century prayer speaks of this life of ours being *fraughted* with adversities. Like barnacles to the bottom of a shippe, the idea of difficulty and adversity attached itself over the years to *fraught*.

You can observe the shift starting to happen as early as Milton. In *Paradise Lost* he uses *fraught* in its literal meaning of 'laden', when he describes Satan, splendidly, flying towards this frail world like 'a weather-beaten vessel full *fraught* with mischievous revenge.' But in *Comus* Milton had used *fraught* in a sense not far removed

51

from our new informal use, when he described the Lady, separated from her brothers in the wild wood, leaning 'her unpillow'd head *fraught* with sad fears' against the rugged bark of some broad elm. I suggest that over the years sad fears became such constant companions of *fraught* that we have started to take them as read.

A parallel shift has happened to the participle 'burdened'. 'Come to me, all you that labour and are burdened', Matthew 11,28 (*Qui laboratis, et onerati estis*). The Authorized Version has: 'Come unto me, all ye that labour and are heavy laden, and I will give you rest,' which is better, as usual. The New English Bible has: 'Come to me, all whose work is hard, whose load is heavy; and I will give you relief,' which is the apotheosis of ecclesiastical banality, as usual.

By some such process of analogy and connotation we have come to use *fraught* absolutely in informal speech to mean that someone is worried and in a tizzy, or that conditions are vexatious. 'You're looking very *fraught*, Philip.' Although *fraught* in its old Merchant Navy sense was peculiarly Scottish, the new vogue use meaning 'harassed' seems peculiarly Southern English and upper-class or U. Eric Partridge and the *OED Supplement* date the shift to some time in the Sixties. Partridge cites *The Long Short Cut* (1968) by Andrew Garve, 'Almost no risks in the early stages ... The end could be a bit *fraught*.' He translates *fraught* as risky or dangerous, and explains that it is elliptical for '*fraught* with danger.'

There is some evidence that takes the new meaning back earlier than the Sixties to that great producer of new English as well as of so much else, the last war. I have been unable to find a printed citation. But I have aged friends who flew in the Battle of Britain who tell me that they used *fraught* in its modern absolute sense as an abbreviated and stiff-upper-lipped form of RAF understatement. If a pilot found himself upside down in cloud, nothing on the clock, and still climbing, and if he came back to earth in one piece, his description of his situation would have been 'pretty *fraught*, old boy.' No doubt he would also have stroked his moustache in a self-depreciating way.

The new use of *fraught* is still too informal to be used in written English, in *The Times* at any rate, I judge, except in the chatty and thistledown parts of the newspaper that lack *gravitas*, or unless it is written by a good writer who fits the colloquial tone of the word to his context. It may be a passing vogue. The new use may become stale and mouldy, and so, boring, and so die. On the other hand, feeling *fraught* may fill a linguistic need in our Age of Anxiety. We shall see. In any case, it is an interesting shift in meaning that is taking place before our very ears.

12/ GAS

How we all keep gassing

Johnny, finding life a bore,
Drank some H_2SO_4.
Johnny's father, an M.D.,
Gave him $CaCO_3$.
Now he's neutralized, it's true,
But he's full of CO_2.

We all know about four-letter words, though we prefer not to use them in print between these chaste covers, unless we have overwhelming cause. But have you ever considered a three-letter word that is similarly fraught with powerful magical and negative connotations? The word is not God, but *gas*.

The word did not evolve naturally. It was invented for his scientific theories by the Swiss physician and alchemist, Philippus Paracelsus (1493–1541), who first had the inspiration of adopting the Ancient Greek word Chaos to mean 'atmospheric air'. In the seventeenth century van Helmont adopted the name for the occult principle that he supposed to be present in all bodies, a kind of air other than the air we breathe. Van Helmont's stroke of genius was to spell the Greek word phonetically, that is, as he and other southern Dutchspeakers would have spelled it, if, knowing no Greek, they had heard it, and had had to write it down in Dutch.

Van Helmont explained his derivation: *Halitum illum* Gas *vocavi, non longe a Chao veterum secretum.* 'I have called this spirit *Gas*, as being not very different from the Chaos of the ancients.' *Gas* or its phonetic equivalent occurs in nearly every language on earth. In nearly every use it has a whiff of unpleasantness.

For some reason we throw in the word *gas* otiosely when we speak or write of substances in the gaseous state, even when that state is normal at ambient temperatures and pressures. We do not say 'copper solid' or 'alcohol liquid'. We may say 'mercury vapour', because vapour is not the normal state of mercury. But listen to a barrister, or read a journalist concerned with Chlorine or Carbon Monoxide. *Gas* is always tacked on as a lurid suffix. Often the whole phrase is prefixed with the adjective 'poisonous', to rub in its sinister sense, although there is no form of either substance that is not poisonous. Poisonous Chlorine *Gas* and Poisonous Carbon Monoxide *Gas* are resounding double tautologies.

Observe the quaint way that popular science books introduce the fact that the air we breathe is a *gas*—even, horror!, a mixture of gases—as much as to say that we are lucky to be alive at all. *Gas* at the dentist's adds to the unpleasantness. *Gas* used figuratively in British English means boastful bombast. *Gas* and gaiters, empty alliteration, are stuff and nonsense, pompousness and verbosity, and nothing to do with Barchester. Dickens invented them in *Nicholas Nickleby*: 'She is come at last—at last—and all is *gas* and gaiters.' '*Gassed* at Mons' (or 'hanging on the old barbed wire', or 'on the wire at Mons') was a British army reply from 1915 on to the query: 'Where is old So-and-So?' There was, of course, no gas used at Mons; nor, come to that, were any barbed-wire entanglements used during the Retreat from Mons.

This last example gives us the clue to the smelly reputation of *Gas*. I think it is largely derived from the use of *Gas*, mostly Chlorine, in the First World War, and the quite unrelated *gas* gangrene, which was a rapidly spreading form of gangrene marked by the evolution of *gas*. The 1914–19 armies had complete and sinister *gas* lexicons: *gas* courses, *gas* masks, *gas* capes, *gas* officers, and so on.

One *gas*, Phosgene, is notable in that it is a chemical compound of Poisonous Chlorine *Gas* and Poisonous Carbon Monoxide *Gas*; and the toxicity of all three *gases* belies the cosy notion sometimes encountered among unscientific donnish people that combinations of noxious substances are often harmless. According to the *gas* manuals, Phosgene smells like musty hay—we wretched townees don't stand a chance with it—and the remedy for it is 'sips of hot sweet tea.'

Gas from the *gas*works, and via *gas* holder and *gas*ometer, is fairly free from the ancestral taint; except that the *gas* oven, before North Sea *Gas*, was a popular method of suicide. *Gas* lighting has an agreeably golden and flickering Victorian glow for me, but I suppose one could associate it with pea-soupers, footfalls echoing behind one, and villainy. Cases of assault sound more savage when done with a length of *gas* piping. *Gaslight* was a Victorian melodrama; and its name was intended to make your flesh creep.

Even British *Gas* Boards have difficulty in bringing themselves to use the word *gas* where it might cause alarm or offence. Someone from the *Gas* Board was explaining to me over the telephone why a *gas* installation was dangerous. She said that 'the product' was coming back into the room. 'The what?' I exclaimed, with some agitation. 'Do you mean *gas* fumes?' She did. In a subsequent letter the preferred euphemism was: '... the back boiler has a defective flue, and as a result the products are entering the lounge.'

Gas has ludicrous as well as sinister connotations. In Peacock's *Nightmare Abbey* (1818) Scythrop, a send-up of Shelley, is 'the author of a treatise, called *Philosophical Gas; or, a Project for a General Illumination of the Human Mind.*' It is impossible to believe that Peacock was unaware of, and did not intend, the ridiculous nature of this title.

It occurs to me, *gassing* away over an idle typewriter, that the evil stink of *gas* may be a peculiarly English phenomenon. To elderly Scots it has a kindlier ring. *Gas*-lamps were lit by the 'leerie' with his tall magic wand, as the children followed him respectfully down the street. 'The *gas*', even if in a fish-tail burner, made reading possible after parents had gone to bed; candles were considered dangerous and damaging to eyesight. *Gassing* was cheerful and harmless gossiping. And what parents disparagingly called 'that *gassy* stuff' was that most delicous of drinks, the American ice cream soda.

In North America *gas* has positive connotations, mainly because of the odd use of *gas* to mean the juice that makes automobiles go. To step on the *gas* is, take it for all in all, a pretty cheerful, or at any rate, a brisk act. In the United States *gas* also means what Britons refer to genteelly as wind. I quote from a book called, uninvitingly, *Be Young with Yoga*: 'Indiscriminate combinations of foods make digestion very difficult and will produce *gas*, bloating, and other discomforts.' I have never been sure if this kind of American *gas* means a fart, or a burp, or both. Do not write. I will look it up for myself. 'What a *gas*!', meaning 'What larks, What fun!', may have come from laughing *gas*. There is a marvellously learned and curious alternative etymology. This suggests that the *gas* in 'What a *gas*!' is Old French, taken to North America and fossilized there. *Gas* appears in Old French as the nominative plural

56

form of *gab*, with a meaning broadly similar to 'jape'. The *OED* points out that it is not easy to make any phonetic connexion between the two words. There was also the verb *gaber*.

If you look at that early exercise in vernacular parody *Le Voyage de Charlemagne à Jérusalem et à Constantinople*, described as an Anglo-Norman poem of the twelfth century, you will find: *'Par Dieu', ço dist l'escolte, 'cist gas est bels et bons ...'.* 'By God, what a *gas*!'

The adjectives retained the plural form also at that date. If you buy this learned and engaging etymology, you are going to have to explain how they retained the plural form *gas* until after Columbus crossed the ocean blue; unless we are going off on a loony voyage after previously unknown Old French explorers who discovered America three centuries before Columbus, in company with St Brendan, the Vikings, the Ancient Egyptians, and the rest of the splendid company who have brought fame and fortune to their sponsors.

It is safer to suppose that *gas* in this sense is, as the terse lexicographers put it, of etym. obsc. We should note, however, its connexion with Irish slang. For example, James Joyce, in *Dubliners*: 'He told me he had brought it (*sc.* a catapult) to have some *gas* with the birds. Mahony used slang freely.'

We should also note, in passing, the use of *GAS* as an acronym in the jargon of Oxford examiners. The chairman, originally from Vienna, of Israel's broadcasting authority was perplexed, on receiving back his first essay while pursuing his legal studies at Oxford, to find the word *gas* frequently penned in the margins. Requesting an explanation, he was told that it stood for, 'German Academic Style.'

It is difficult elsewhere to find humour or poetry in the melancholy three-letter word. Erasmus Darwin, the grandfather and precursor of Evolution Darwin, made an attempt, in the only poem I know of addressed to a *gas*, about the birth of KNO_3:

'Hence orient Nitre owes its sparkling birth,
And with prismatic crystals gems the earth,
O'er tottering domes the filmy foliage crawls,
Or frosts with branching plumes the mould'ring walls;
As woos Azotic *Gas* the virgin Air,
And veils in crimson clouds the yielding fair.'

13/ GHOST-WORDS

Some skeletons in the dictionary

> I've only to pick up a newspaper and I seem to see ghosts gliding between the lines.
> Henrik Ibsen, *Ghosts*, Act 2

Some words are ghosts. Others are merely superannuated. Your true ghost word is a very rare beast indeed, a wild impossible chimera that never before entered into the heart of man to conceive. It has no existence outside the pages of a dictionary. And even there it does not last for long. The 1952 edition of *Chambers Twentieth Century Dictionary* defined 'ghost-word' agreeably as: 'A word that has originated in the blunder of a scribe or printer—common in dictionaries.' Alas, the last three words of the definition have been cut by subsequent humourless editors.

The most famous example of a ghost-word in English is the supposedly active verb, *to foupe*, which Dr Johnson defined in his *Dictionary* as 'to drive with sudden impetuosity', and glossed, 'a word out of use.' As an example, Samuel gave a passage from Camden's *Remaines* in Philemon Holland's elegant translation: 'We pronounce, by the confession of strangers, as smoothly and moderately as any of the northern nations, who *foupe* their words out of the throat with fat and full spirits.'

Alas and dammit, the word *foupe* and the definition are ghosts; though the gloss is strictly true, since the word has never been in use. Johnson misread the long 's' in the citation. What Philemon had actually written was 'soupe', which may have been your common-or-arden minestrone, or more probably was an obscure variant spelling of 'swoop', meaning 'to utter forcibly.' In the five editions of the *Remaines* between 1614 and 1637 the word was misprinted *foupe*.
58

After I had discussed the ghost-word, to *foupe*, in *The Times*, I was surprised to receive a letter from the Prime Minister's Office in Bridgetown, Barbados. John Michael Geoffrey Manningham Adams, then Prime Minister of Barbados, and a sharp-eyed word-smith and logophile, wrote to point out that the ghost *fouping* still walks abroad in his island in coarsely material form. Until then it had been assumed that *foupe* had no solid existence in the English lexicon apart from Dr Johnson's error. But it lives in Barbados, where Mr Adams took it to be a purely local coinage, usually found sprayed on walls.

For a very long time the word '*foop*' (usually spelt this way, to judge from the consensus of graffiti, but admitting the variants *foup* and *foupe*) has been considered by the more uninhibited and out-spoken citizens of Barbados to be the exclusively Barbadian variant of the other sexual four-letter word beginning with 'f' in popular use in the rest of the English-speaking world. The Prime Minister and other Barbadians are persuaded that their word is more euphonious and sounds less aggressive than the British and American alternative.

There are minor distinctions between the two words. No Barbadian uses *fooping* as an intensifying adjective. And the philo-logically perspicacious Prime Minister puts forward his theory, the Adams *Foop* Hypothesis, that only human beings *foop*, and generally human beings of opposite sexes. The student of graffiti will observe that the only four-letter word beginning with 'f' that is ever scratched or painted on walls in Barbados is *foop*. You can see it *passim* on the corner of Culloden Road and Beckles Road, and in two or three other grand canvases for graffiti-artists in Bridgetown.

After Mr Adams and I had trotted our hobby-horse for a while, the *Beacon*, the Barbados Labour Party's newspaper, put forward the engaging but extravagant suggestion that *foop* in Barbados may be a living descendant of Dr Johnson's ghost-word *foupe*, which he defined as 'driving with sudden impetuosity.' I suggest that Francis Barber, born a slave in Jamaica, not Barbados, must have transmitted the word to some Barbadian uncle. Be that as it may not, it adds to the stock of linguistic knowledge and harmless pleasure to learn that the old ghost word to *foupe* has materialized in Barbados.

Skeat was using the term 'ghost-word' as long ago as 1886. The other classic specimen is 'Dord', which made its spectral appearance in early printings of the Second (1934) Edition of the Merriam

Webster unabridged, where it was defined as a word for 'density' in physics and chemistry. What had happened was that the entry 'D or d' had been telescoped and misread as a single word. Instead of realizing that this meant an alternative, 'D or d', the upper-case and lower-case abbreviations for density, the printer contracted them into the ghost-word 'Dord'. It is undecided whether or not there has ever been an instance of this ghost-word appearing outside a dictionary, on a wall in Barbados or elsewhere. All argument is against it; but all hope is for it.

'Phantomnation' is an agreeable and useful word, you would think. It has been defined by lexicographers and critics as, 'the appearance of a phantom; an illusion.' It is, appropriately, a ghost-word. It came from Pope's *Odyssey*, X, 627, 'The Phantome-nations of the dead.' An editor with a Procrustean attitude to writing compounds published it as 'phantomnation'; and the critics picked up the ghost-word with avidity.

Another famous ghost is 'howl', defined by lexicographers as a Scottish spelling of 'hovel'. In fact, a printer had altered Robert Louis Stevenson's 'howf', a Scottish dialect word for a shelter.

I also greatly like 'momblishness', explained as 'muttering talk.' If it did not exist, somebody ought to invent it. It is another ghost-word. It was created by a misunderstanding of the rare Anglicized French term 'ne moubliemies', sc. forget-me-nots. But king of the phantasmagoria, especially in Barbados, is *foupe*.

Superannuated words are not ghosts, but they do not sound healthy. However, the flux of language is so unpredictable that it is dangerous to predict which words are superannuated or going out of use. Swift attacked 'mob' as a miserable contraction from 'mobile vulgus', and a superannuated vulgarity that was going out of use. In 1758 Launcelot Temple published a tract entitled *Sketches or Essays on Various Subjects*, which included a sketch 'Of Super-annuated Words'. In this class Temple listed: 'encroach'; 'purport'; 'froward'; and 'swerve'. 'Wittol', on the other hand (*OED*, 'a man who is aware of and complaisant about the infidelity of his wife; a contented cuckold'), Temple judged to be somewhat old-fashioned, but much used, and with a long life ahead of it. Either Launcelot Temple was a rotten philologist, or some superannuated words found a new lease of life, while other robust words suddenly faded away.

Poltergeist words change their meanings through misapprehension, with a sudden loud noise. For example, 'scarifying' is widely used today as a colloquial synonym for 'scaring'. Until now, what it used to mean was 'covering with scratches or scars', as when scoring the bark of a tree, or breaking up the surface of a road.

For another example, those who package frozen foods and cook Chinese food err when they suppose that 'crispy' is primarily a friendlier and more tempting way of saying 'crisp'. That old poltergeist word, 'crispy', used to mean curly, wavy, and undulated, as in crispy hair. I have met hairy crispy noodles in my chop suey, but I doubt whether that sort of 'crispy' was intended in that way.

14/ HALCYON

Halcyon days are here again

Expect Saint Martin's summer, halcyon days.
Shakespeare, *Henry VI, part 1*, I, 2, 131

In the 1980s *halcyon* has suddenly become a vogue bird. No piece of journalism or broadcasting that wants to sound trendy these days should fail to include at least one reference to those goddamned kingfishers. *Halcyon* is the hottest vogue word for politicians and journalists who want to be with-it: it is as contagious as fowl pest. In a few years we shall grow bored with it, and move on to something else. But, for the moment, everything is *halcyon*.

As often with words that suddenly become fashionable, it is changing its meaning slightly as it is popularized. People like the look of the shiny new word, pick it up, and start dropping it into their discourse without making sure exactly what it means, so vexing pedants and providing amusement and copy for those of us who observe and record the changing language. It is evident that many of those now using *halcyon* to add a touch of class to their writing or speaking take the word to mean something like 'in the good old days'.

I was finally moved to write an article about the matter in the winter of 1981–82, when one day I found no fewer than four *halcyons* nesting on the Letters Page of *The Times* and the Features Page opposite, which we call the Op Ed Page in these bustling times, now that it is no longer necessarily the Left Centre Page. Our Moscow Correspondent, that careful and professional scribe, used *halcyon* as an exact metaphor to describe the peaceful days of détente. But the other sightings suggested either that the user had not quite understood the meaning of *halcyon*, or that its meaning was being changed to meet a new linguistic need. For example, one of our correspondents described Britain in 1879 as *halcyon*.

I reached for my dictionary of dates, and discovered that 1879 was the year in which Britain invaded Afghanistan, British breech-loading rifles wiped out the Zulu nation, the War of the Pacific began, the Tay Bridge collapsed, and Mary Baker Eddy invented (sorry, chartered) the Church of Christ Scientist. And, apart from all that, the weather was terrible. I doubt whether 1879 can be classified as *halcyon* in the extreme acceptance of the word without some risk of terminological inexactitude.

It has become a cliché to refer to the *halcyon* days just before the First World War, when in fact they were overcast with intense domestic political conflict and international uncertainty. But the jolliest example I have come across so far is in an advertisement for a brand of Citizens' Band radio, which has died the death in the United Kingdom, instead of washing over us as it has in the United States, interfering with police and medical communications, and polluting the waves. But some of its curious jargon has infected British English. The advertisement runs: 'For CB'ers who want something a little more advanced, the HALCYON CONDOR is on its way.' Now there is a flying oxymoron, if ever I saw one. I had a charming letter from the charmingly Christian-named Mrs Halcyon McLaren, which we published under the headline: 'Shall I call thee bird?' I suppose that the answer to that question is that Mrs McLaren was a Wren in the war.

The new meaning of *halcyon* seems to be what Lauritz Melchior used to bellow from *The Student Prince* in tenor tones of melted toffee:

'Golden Days, in the sunshine of our happy youth;
Golden Days, full of innocence and full of tru-u-uth.'

Halcyon, as fashionably overused in the Eighties, harks back nostalgically to some notional Golden Age when things went well, the trains ran on time, and people were content. Historical memo to self: they never did, and they never were.

What *halcyon* originally meant was for the birds. It is the Greek word for a kingfisher, a compound derived from *hals* (salt, and thus a poetic word for the sea) and *kuon* (conceiving, going broody, nesting). The Greeks, particularly the Greek colonials in Sicily, believed that the kingfisher laid its eggs on the surface of the sea, and incubated for fourteen days, during which time the sea was exceptionally calm.

> 'Amidst our arms as quiet you shall be
> As *halcyon* brooding on a winter's sea.'

There you go: an exact simile from Dryden, with modest smile, the master of the middle style.

The Greeks made a myth out of their avian theory. *Halcyon* or *Alcyone*, daughter of Aeolus, the keeper of the winds, was married to Ceyx, the mortal King of Thessaly. In spite of his influential windy connexions, Ceyx was drowned in a storm at sea, and his dead body was washed back to shore, where his wife was waiting for him. *Alcyone* was so distressed that she took the extravagant step of turning into a bird, skimmed along the surface of the sea, enfolded the corpse with her new wings, and kissed it with her beak. The Gods take pity and turn Ceyx into a kingfisher also. All roses. They mate. *Alcyone* broods. Aeolus locks up winds to protect his grandchildren in their eggs. If you must go to sea, choose *Halcyon* Days.

There is an alternative version of the myth. There usually is. This one is given in Ovid's *Metamorphoses*, that brilliant menagerie of men and other beasts changing their shapes and sizes. In this account of the matter *Halcyon* is so much in love with her husband that she commits an act of hubris by calling herself Hera and him Zeus. This naturally vexes that curmudgeon, Olympian Zeus, who sends a thunderstorm to drown Ceyx, the husband. *Alcyone* is so upset that she jumps into the sea and drowns herself. Some pitying god turns them both into kingfishers, or, according to a variant, *Alcyone* into a kingfisher and Ceyx into a seagull. The gods still make the seas calm for them to nest at the winter solstice—hence your *Halcyon* Days.

In the myth, *Halcyon*, as well as being the harbinger of fine weather, is the symbolic type for whatever is the female of an uxorious husband. The word you are looking for, Philip, is the rare and meritorious one, maritorious.

The story is, of course, partly guano. The legend of the kingfisher's floating nest has no foundation in natural history. Your *halcyon* builds no kind of nest at all, but lays its eggs in a hole by the waterside. However, myth is not nonsense. It expresses ritual and religious truth. The *Halcyon* myth refers to the birth of a new sacred king at the winter solstice—after the queen, who represents his mother,

64

the Moon Goddess, has conveyed the old king's corpse to a sepulchral island. Or so says Robert Graves, and I potently and powerfully believe him.

This may seem a bit esoteric in light of the modern vogue use of *halcyon* to mean, 'in the good old days, when I was young, and you could buy a four-course dinner with wine for half-a-crown.' But it is interesting as an example of a word in the process of changing its meaning. It shows what we have lost now that the classics and classical mythology are no longer generally taught in British schools. It is impossible to get the most out of Western literature and art without knowing about birds like *Halcyon*.

The myth and the word have resonated in European literature for more than twenty centuries. Remember Milton in *Hymn to the Nativity*: 'While birds of calm sit brooding on the charmed wave.' Remember John Keats in *Endymion*:

> 'O magic sleep! O comfortable bird
> That broodest o'er the troubled sea of the mind
> Till it is hushed and smooth.

Remember Christina Georgina Rossetti:

> 'My heart is like a singing bird
> Whose nest is in a watered shoot ...
> My heart is like a rainbow shell
> That paddles in a *halcyon* sea.'

Pretend that you can remember the obscure poet, Wild:

> The peaceful king fishers are met together
> About the deck and prophesie calm weather.'

Let us not forget the comfortable bird, nor completely lose the sense of calm weather in our vogue use of her name.

15/ HOLES IN THE LANGUAGE

Where there's a will, there's a word

> Every living language, like the perspiring bodies of living creatures, is in perpetual motion and alteration; some words go off, and become obsolete; others are taken in, and by degrees grow into common use; or the same word is inverted to a new sense and notion, which in tract of time makes as observable a change in the air and features of a language as age makes in the lines and mien of a face.
>
> Richard Bentley, *Dissertation Upon the Epistles of Phalaris*, 1697

English has by far the largest vocabulary of any tongue that has babbled since the boys started to build a tower to reach unto heaven on a plain in the land of Shinar. We may not deploy it as profusely as we could. I suspect that English may have fewer words in actual use than French or German. A good yardstick is to compare an issue of *The Times* with one of *Le Figaro*. But what English has more of than any other language is words available in the lexicon, and idioms, i.e. expressions of shades of meaning by the placing of words. In spite of this profusion, there are still blanks in English, black holes, and meanings that are better expressed in other languages.

We have no single word for *Schadenfreude*. Nor, for that matter, has any other language apart from German, with the single exception of Hungarian. We say that that deficiency arises because the English are such decent, agreeable people. The Germans say that there is a hole in the language, and that it shows that the English are singularly lacking in self-awareness. They point out, in addition, that English is the only language in which the first person singular pronoun is capitalized, in this respect comparing unfavourably with German. No translation of *Schadenfreude* is adequate. 'Malignant joy' and 'malicious joy' do not hit the bull's eye. 'Pleasure in disaster' is better, but still sounds too much like an abnormality. 'Thrill in disaster' is the best I can do, but still artificial and contrived, and inappropriate for translating into English Alfred Polgar's immortal

Schadenfreude, schöner Götterfunken,
Tochter aus dem Café Elysium!

We shall just have to live with the black hole in our language, and stick to *Schadenfreude*.

There is no way that one can say *mutatis mutandis* in English without intolerable periphrasis. The Académie française accepts *en faisant les changements nécessaires*, which is as good an example of *périphrase* as any.

We need an adjective in English to fill another gap. We fill it at present with an illogical use of such words as 'extraordinary', 'strange', 'odd', and 'rum'. Here are some examples. 'Aren't people extraordinary?' A person can be extraordinary; but it is quite impossible for *people* to be extraordinary. 'Isn't it odd how everyone seems to think ...?' If everybody does it, it cannot be odd, baby. 'Strange that nobody ever replies to such appeals.' If no one does, the absence of reply must be familiar, not strange. 'Extraordinary name, Smith, really: I mean you find it coupled with absolutely anything...' Isn't it odd that everybody says this kind of thing? I certainly do.

I suppose, hoisting the philosopher's black flag, we might say that these words need not mean 'unusual'; they may also mean 'surprising'. And there is nothing odd or strange about finding it *surprising* that people are not more intelligent, or that nobody ever replies to such appeals. For that matter, there is not any logical or linguistic impropriety in finding it surprising that nobody has a tail, or that women do not lay eggs. (It would certainly ease a great many of our current social problems if they did.) To find something surprising does not imply that one must have experienced an actual shock of surprise on discovering it, or that it must be statistically unusual; only that one must have reasons for supposing that it could have been otherwise. Thus a biologist or zoologist might find it surprising that nobody has a tail, because he can give scientific reasons for thinking that humans (or some humans) might have been expected to have tails. Such a man would not have been actually surprised to discover the absence of tails among humans, for he probably knew that humans are tailless before he came to regard this as surprising. OK, back to your tub, Diogenes.

But 'surprising' does not make explicit, though perhaps it retains,

67

the slight nuance of disapproval that is present in most of these uses of 'extraordinary' and its fellows used to fill the black hole in the language. Indeed, it is not always slight. 'Aren't people extra-ordinary?' is close to 'extraordinary conduct!', where the point is not the statistical infrequency of such conduct, but its impropriety. And, of course, I may quite legitimately say that it is *surprising* that nobody achieves a satisfactory standard of courtesy, or of intel-ligence, or of anything else that lends itself to the notion of standards or ideals. (We have to avoid the word 'norm', since this also loses itself in the general confusion that exists between the average and the ideal. Is this peculiarly English? Are we the only people whose speech-forms are riddled with the assumption that what is unusual must be improper, if not downright sinister?) Enough. I surrender. Philosophy is a route of many roads leading from nowhere to nothing, and we have followed that one for long enough into a black hole of English.

There is a similar rum illogicality in the universal journalistic misuse of mean/means/meant/will mean. For example, from the romantic topic of the decade: 'Lord Spencer's friendship with the Royal Family *meant* that the Queen is godmother to ...' Well, I see what he means, but, really, it didn't *mean* anything of the sort. Sentences mean. Symbols can mean. Such expressions as 'the mean-ing of life', or 'on this view it is hard to see what human existence can mean' are nothing but sophistry and illusion, and should be committed to the flames.

George Mikes, that most native of aliens, who writes better English than most of us, points out another black hole in the language. He declares that there is one expression he has particularly missed for half a century, ever since he tried to learn our extraordinary language. If it existed it would be 'how manieth?'—the equivalent of *wievielte* in German; or *hanyadik* in Hungarian. When one gets into a lift, the person nearest to the buttons may ask, 'which floor?', which is a reasonable substitute to help one over the deficiency. But, if you want to know how manieth child a chap is in his family, you have to ask: 'Any brothers or sisters?' Then, when he replies that he has seven brothers and eight sisters, you have to carry on with your prolix interrogation: 'Are you the eldest among the boys?'

Not many languages have 'how manieth'. It does not exist in Greek or Latin, nor in most of the Romance languages. Though *hanyadik* comes quite trippingly on the Hungarian tongue, as does *quantième* on the French, the German *wievielte* sounds pretty laboured in the question of the children's comparative ages. 'Which floor?' does not admit misunderstanding, and will serve. The question about the children's ages should not be asked by decent people, anyway.

There are other gaps in the language, the most obvious one to feminists being the lack of a sexually neutral pronoun to do the work of 'he or she', 'her or him', 'his or hers', and so on. Enthusiasts have tried to create a unisex pronoun. But that is not the way that language generally works, though it has worked with the appellation Ms, as a handle to give a woman without going into whether she is married or not. One of the embarrassing jobs of a newspaper reporter used to be to ask a woman whether she was married or not, in order that he or she could style her Mrs or Miss. Ms may be artificial and horrid, but it serves a worthy purpose. What in fact is happening about the unisex pronoun is that 'their' is becoming a singular pronoun without gender. 'Everybody should do their own thing without harassment about their gender' may be a ghastly solecism, but it is rapidly becoming idiomatic, in spite of the grunts of m.c.p.s. It is, at any rate, less cumbersome than, 'everyone should do his or her own thing, without harassment about her or his gender.'

Another remarkable hole in a language that evolved, like almost all languages, in a pastoral and agricultural society, is that we have no singular for the word 'cattle'. We have to say heifer/cow or ox/bullock/bull, which is cumbersome and lumbering. We can see how this gap arose. Cattle is a variant of chattel. Its original general sense 'wealth, property' became narrowed to 'movable property', especially as typified by livestock. This has been the only application in modern times, except in the legal phrase 'goods and chattels', a translation of the Anglo-Latin *bona et catalla*. In the agricultural midlands 'a beast' is used as the singular of cattle, being specifically bovine and singular. 'Beasts' is also a collective plural. There used to be another perfectly good singular for cattle, a 'beef'. It fell into disuse in the nineteenth century. Perhaps we should accept that if a language loses a word, it means that it does not need it. Perhaps we should accept that if the need is there, we will create new words to fill the black holes in our language.

Here is another curious hole in the language. We have no word in English to describe something annexed to the vertical, corresponding to 'sprawling' or 'recumbent' in relation to the horizontal. You would have thought that need would have evolved a participial adjective to do the job. But it has not. And in the absence of a suitable word we make do with 'lie' and 'lying'.

For example, a local newspaper carried an illustration with the caption: 'The proud plaque that *lies* on the wall of the hospital.' (The plaque is said to be proud because it is crowned with the Prince of Wales's Feathers.) Strictly, the plaque is not lying, but stuck vertically to the wall: an awkward position for lying for all except the most advanced yogis.

A recent pop song, *I'm Not In Love*, sung by a group called 'Ten C.C.', has a line explaining why the boy has hung a photograph of the girl on his wall, even though he is not in love with her. It is 'to hide a nasty stain that's *lying* there.' The building industry uses 'cladding' to mean materials of any kind used as a vertical covering for a wall. From this noun, the industry has invented the intransitive verb 'to clad'; but has so far fought shy of 'cladded.'

More possible black holes: we have no antonym to the Civil Service cliché of a high-flyer. Would he be a depth-plumber, a ground hugger, or a hedge-hopper (one who escapes observation and circumvents control)? The world of education has invented the horrid and illogical 'low achiever', which is as close as English comes at present to the opposite of a high-flyer.

Why is there no adjective from the noun 'integrity'? There used to be one, 'integrous', but it faded away, presumably because 'honest' is easier to say and spell.

A Member of Parliament recently complained that his requests for a particular course of action had been treated with 'complete ignoral.' Do we need the word? Are the jocular antonyms 'gruntled', 'hevilled', 'couth', and 'kempt' going to be made respectable by adoption into the formal lexicon of English? Is there a black hole for a word to convey exactly the sense of the French *de trop*, when one feels out of place at a gathering? 'Superfluous' is too mild; 'intruder' too strong; 'spare' too colloquial; 'not wanted on voyage' and 'surplus to requirements' too facetious. 'Gooseberry' comes close, but is too restricted.

These are puzzling black holes; but not beyond all conjecture. If there is a need, we shall find a word for it.

16/ JINGO FIGHTING TALK

*I have always been against the Pacifists during the quarrel,
and against the Jingoes at its close (Sir Winston Churchill)*

> in every language even deafanddumb
> thy sons acclaim your glorious name by gorry
> by jingo by gee by gosh by gum.
> [e.e. cummings]

War changes the language as well as the landscape. It would be
remarkable indeed if the most terrible and decisive of human
activities did not affect the way we talk about the world. The small
war that Britain and the Argentine fought in 1982 in the Falklands/
Malvinas has already started to leave its mark on both languages.
It brought us from the ski plains of Scandinavia the verb *to yomp*,
that splendidly onomatopoeic Royal Marine word for marching bag
and baggage across country. It brought us the *Falklands Spirit*, so
ardently invoked by Britain's Boadicea prime minister. It brought
us the dreaded *Exocet* missile, which has already been picked up
and widely used metaphorically by those magpies of the language,
politicians and journalists. It is not an elegant metaphor. It seems
to me flash, vulgar, in bad taste, and unlikely to find a permanent
place in the language. The French will soon invent something even
nastier.

But the etymology of *Exocet* is irresistible. It is no barbarous
acronym, but a word of impeccable classical antecedents. The Greek
word transliterated *exokoitos* meant 'sleeping out'; according to
Hesychius it was applied to an unknown fish said to sleep out of
the water. Oppian observed that it was the laziest of fishes, for it
lay around the shore sleeping all day, and went about its business,
such as it was, by night. Others called the fish Adonis. In the
eighteenth century, however, Linnaeus appropriated its name to give
to the flying fish, still scientifically known as *Exocoetus volitans*.

Hence the French, who show a great deal more imagination in their military nomenclature than we do, took the name for their expensive and lethal missile that skims the surface of the sea.

The Falklands War brought back a lot of *jingoism*, at any rate in the spoken and written word, and maybe even in the real world out there. *Jingo* is a slippery value word. One man's *jingo* is another man's patriot is another man's trendy wet lefty.

Every schoolboy and girl used to know how the exclamation came to acquire its faint descriptive meaning, from the refrain of a music hall song composed by G. W. Hunt and top of the pops in 1878.

'We don't want to fight, but, by jingo, if we do,
We've got the ships, we've got the men, we've got the money too.
We've fought the Bear before, and while Britons shall be true,
The Russians shall not have Constantinople.'
Rabble-rousing stuff, though not very well scanned.

For those whose school history is fading at the edges, the word came into the lexicon of political slang as a boo-word during the Balkan crisis over the alleged Turkish persecution of Christians in their empire. On the left, Gladstone, threatening to bundle the Turks out of Europe 'bag and baggage', and so giving hacks another useful rhetorical cliché. Gladstone cribbed it from Shakespeare, the originator of most of the best clichés. *As You Like It* III, 2, 172, Touchstone: 'Come, shepherd, let us make an honourable retreat; though not with bag and baggage, yet with scrip and scrippage.' *The Winter's Tale* I, 2, 204, Leontes: 'I will let in and out the enemy with bag and baggage.'

On the right, Disraeli, backed up as usual by his Queen, who threatened the Russians with war if they did not halt the flow of 'volunteers' into Turkey. He felt that the Russians were less concerned with the fate of the Christian minorities than with expanding their territory at the expense of the Turks.

For a time Disraeli was forced into neutrality. But when Russia invaded Turkey in 1878, he sent in the British fleet, and helped to arrange what he called 'peace with honour', another useful catchphrase of martial rhetoric. Cicero coined it in Latin; Shakespeare brought it into English. *Coriolanus*, V, 5:
'We have made peace
With no less honour to the Antiates
Than shame to the Romans.'
Jingo did not spring from nowhere into the lexicon of political abuse in 1878. It was first recorded in the seventeenth century in

the patter of conjurors, usually as *hey jingo* or *high jingo*, to summon the mysterious appearance of something. *Hey presto* for purist conjurors is what you exclaim when you make something disappear.

Then *By Jingo!* came to be used as a vigorous asseveration, for example in 1694 as a translation of *par Dieu!* in Rabelais. I suspect that it may have a euphemistic connexion with diffidence about naming the deity, as it begins with 'j'. Jee Whiz is clearly a euphemism for Jesus.

Jingo has strong Scottish connexions. Cartoon characters in the comic strips of publications of the D. C. Thomson empire of Dundee regularly ejaculate at each other such phrases as 'O *jings*, oor Wullie.' My impression is that outside strip cartoons it would be difficult for a modern Scot to cry *Jingo* without irony or antiquarianism.

Jingo has become a useful tool in the political kitbag to describe advocates of a bellicose policy in dealing with foreign powers. Its near-synonym in French has had an equally curious history, being derived from a certain Nicolas Chauvin, a French fusilier born at Rochefort, whose simple-minded heroism and devotion to Napoleon made his name a byword, and eventually an eponymous word in its own right. Its brilliant adoption by the feminist movement has transferred chauvinism from the shooting wars to the war between the sexes, where it flourishes in such phrases as male chauvinist pig, or m.c.p.

Task Force, a pleonastic American hyperbole, was confirmed in British English idiom by the Falklands War. I have a friend who saw the phrase arrive. He was serving with the Royal Navy in Iceland in 1942 when they received a coded message from our new American allies: 'North Atlantic Task Force arriving at dusk on the fourteenth.' They had never heard of a Task Force before, and their American dictionaries and code books were no help. Then, on the evening of the fourteenth, into Reykjavik steamed a cruiser and a couple of destroyers, and they realized that Task Force was just an inflated name for force, flotilla, squadron, detachment, and so on. I suppose that we can justify its semantics by saying that it is or should be a force designated for a particular task. But the principal reason that it is preferred to duller alternatives is that it sounds more impressive, in the same way that one used to dress up one's regiments of Guards in scarlet uniforms and tall hats to make them appear more formidable to the opposition.

The first full-scale British war for thirty years revived ancient idiom and slang in the military lexicon. *Rookie* meaning a raw recruit experienced a resurrection as remarkable as that of Lazarus. I had always assumed that it was of American origin in the First World War, with all those doughboys. Why doughboy? Nobody knows. Maybe because the American infantry had large globular brass buttons like small doughnuts. Maybe because they had white belts and had to clean them with 'dough' made of pipe clay.

But your *rookie*, who ran wild over the front pages of the *Sun* and the *Daily Mirror* in the spring and summer of 1982, is no American. He is as British as the tommy. His first appearance in literature was in Kipling's *Barrack-Room Ballads*, published in 1892, 'so 'ark an' 'eed you rookies, which is always grumblin' sore.' It was widely adopted as the term for a raw recruit (the best guess is that the word is a corruption of 'recruit') or a novice at some other sport as well as war. The Falklands War revived *rookies* and *jingoes* dramatically. War is an infrequent activity these days. Accordingly, as well as creating its new jargon, it brings back to life atavistic jargon as well as atavistic emotions.

17/ MATHEMATICS

The wrong end of the equation

Mathematics contains much that will neither hurt one if one does not know it nor help one if one does know it.
J. B. Mencken, *De charlataneria eruditorum*, II, 1715

Technical words lose their edge because of loose use by amateurs. This is particularly so with the technical words of a discipline like mathematics, which most of us find difficult and often vexing. We have it from the horse's mouth of Bertrand Russell, a sound mathematician, that maths is the only science where one never knows what one is talking about, nor whether what is said is true. If Lord Russell also felt that, what hope is there for the rest of us?

Parameter is the classic recent example of a mathematical term that has been hazily apprehended, widely misunderstood, and popularized. A lot of us mathematical dunces seem to think that it is merely an impressive alternative to a perimeter.

I detect increasing evidence that we magpie and hyperbole-hungry journalists are picking up another impressive mathematical term, and, as usual, getting hold of the wrong end of the equation. That last sentence is a good example of sloppy journalistic use of a technical term: an equation cannot have a wrong end; by definition, both ends are equal.

The words are *exponential* and *exponentially*, and they are becoming very fashionable, to lend a touch of scientific class to one's prose. In maths *exponential* is one of the most widely diffused terms, and has complex but exact meanings. In journalism the meanings are blunted. For example, it has become fashionable to say or write that something is increasing *exponentially*, where the context makes clear that all that we mean is that it is increasing faster than we had expected.

Generally the essence of *exponential* change (increase or decrease)

75

is that the rate of increase (or decrease) is directly proportional to the size (expressed as a number) of whatever it is that is increasing (or decreasing). It follows that the rate of increase (or decrease) must itself be changing simultaneously with the change. *Exponential* growth is a steeply rising curve. Speaking journalistically, the more the merrier: the less, increasingly the slower.

Capital at compound interest, and population (if you do nothing to check it, and let things rip) grow (roughly) *exponentially*, i.e., at a rate that bears a constant proportion to the instantaneous capital value or the present number of the population. Precise examples of *exponential* growth or decay are radioactive disintegration, and transient changes in temperature governed by Newton's law of cooling.

We can express this mathematically, if we must. The concept of *exponential* function in mathematics is bound up, *inter alia*, with the idea of inverse proportion. Essentially, this means, for a function of two variables, that a small change in one variable results in a relatively large change in the other variable. The exponential function of A is the limit of the quantity $(1 + A \div n)$ multiplied by itself n times, the limit being that reached when n is increased indefinitely.

Having stepped in the bloody business so far, returning were as tedious as go o'er. In pure mathematical language, the precise nature of what counts as *exponential* can scarcely be understood by the non-mathematician. The *exponential* function is precisely the inverse function of the natural logarithm, and its full mathematical properties can be said to be complex under different branches of mathematics.

In linear algebra, for instance, it is necessary to grasp the technical ideas of infinity and limit before the *exponential* function is properly understood. In analytical geometry, the concept of mapping becomes essential. It is perhaps interesting (or, at any rate, daunting) to note that the definition of the general *exponential* function in analytical geometry goes as follows: 'For any prescribed positive number A, the general *exponential* function is defined to be the composite function e xLogA, viz., the magnification (Log A)x followed by the natural *exponential* function.'

Phew. If we are going to insist that laymen should use *exponential* exactly, in its mathematical sense, I doubt that it would ever be consciously and correctly used by any non-mathematician. We cannot insist on that. Words cannot be declared private property and out of bounds to the uninitiated. They are always going to be picked

76

up and used metaphorically and in other transferred ways. But any old increase, which is not accelerating, cannot be described, even loosely, as *exponential*. However, because of the impressiveness and difficulty of the word, it is. It is a silly vogue that blunts a sharp word. I am resolved never to use it again.

It is not surprising that we get *exponential* wrong. We have been getting the much simpler mathematical term *lowest common denominator* wrong in political speeches and articles for years. Here is a recent and typical example from an article about Zimbabwe: 'The new standard would be the *lowest common denominator*, and the whites would go to the wall.' I can see what it means in the woolly journalistic sense of *lowest common denominator*. But it is impossible to establish any logical link between its presumed meaning in this context, and the arithmetical term that we learnt about when we were doing vulgar fractions at school. The *denominator* is the divisor of a fraction, as 3 in $\frac{2}{3}$ and 4 in $\frac{3}{4}$. Sometimes, but not always, sense can be restored to the amateur misuse of *denominators* by reading *highest common factor* for *lowest common denominator*. It would in the example at the beginning of this paragraph. I think that the nonsensical substitution has become commonplace because *lowest common denominator* is generally used in a pejorative sense; and to us silly non-mathematicians 'high' equals good, while 'low' equals bad.

Words that become popular with the general public may provide clues to social changes in the world outside the dictionary. The great vogue for 'situation' in the Seventies reflected the *exponen*—(no, forget it), the rapid increase in students and graduates of sociology. It may also have reflected a fashion for describing events without allocating human causes (strike situation, conflict situation)—a symptom of defeatism and fear of personal responsibility. Its misuse in industry, which was epidemic, reflected a loss of belief, and confusion about where authority lay.

The percolation of mathematical and computer terms into everyday consciousness and particularly into the vocabulary of action and achievement in our working lives is a recent and significant development. It is clearly connected with the growth of the new technology. I hope that it also indicates an affinity with that technology and the benefits that the third Industrial Revolution can bring.

18/ MOLE

Making a mountain out of a molehill

> A prince should have a spy to observe what is necessary, and what is unnecessary,
> in his own as well as in his enemy's country. He is the king's eye; and he who
> hath him not is blind.
> *The Hitopadesa*, III, c. 500

The London evening newspaper (we have only one in these hard
times) announced portentously the other day on a placard: STEEL
MOLE SPEAKS. It stopped me in my tracks in Fleet Street. In
fact the advertisement was referring to an employee of British Steel
who had furtively passed confidential documents of his employers
to a television programme. This vivid new metaphor of a mole as
a spy in the enemy camp, burrowing away underground and usually
unspeaking, was made popular by the spy thrillers of John le Carré,
particularly *Tinker, Tailor, Soldier, Spy*. It has burrowed its way
into the public imagination and the Balaam-baskets of sub-editors
who invent headlines.

A Mr A. J. Mole wrote engagingly complaining about the way
that le Carré and Sir Alec Guinness (who played Smiley brilliantly
on the box) have abused his surname to mean sneak, spy, or even
informer. He asked me to redress the balance.

Apart from Kenneth Grahame's *The Wind in the Willows*, from
which Mr Mole is imprinted as an endearing if bumbling goody
into the subconscious of British children, the mole has generally
had a bad press. In the Authorized Version, Leviticus lists the mole
as an unclean abomination, along with the ferret, the snail, and others.
The translators of the *New English Bible* are, no doubt, more
accurate, but, again no doubt, more boring when they render the
Hebrew with pedantry about the jerboa, the sand-gecko, and the
wall-gecko. In one of his testy fulminations, Isaiah prophesies that
when the Lord comes to shake the earth, a man, not surprisingly

in the circumstances, shall cast his idols of silver and his idols of gold to the moles and to the bats. The gnomes of the *New English Bible* again spoil the poetry by explaining smugly that Isaiah meant dung-beetles, not moles.

Dr Kenneth Mellanby's definitive work on the family *Talpidae*, *The Mole*, states firmly: 'Moles hate their own species,' and quotes from W. G. Lewis (1828): 'This solitary, mischievous animal appears adapted to a life of darkness. Although it is doomed to hunt its prey under ground, and usually denied the cheering light of the sun, yet no animal appears fatter nor has a more sleek and glossy skin.' Dr Mellanby points out that while the relevant Government departments designate the mole as a 'pest' or even as 'vermin', the animal 'has his defenders who think that, under some circumstances, he does more good than harm.'

King William III, Dutch Billy, would not have been one of them. He is supposed to have caught his death of cold from a fall caused by his favourite horse, Sorrel, stumbling over a molehill in Hampton Court Park. Jacobites toasted 'the little gentleman in black velvet' for toppling the king they regarded as the usurper.

Mole proverbs are generally unflattering, and concerned with short-sightedness, as in: 'blind as a mole'; 'Argus abroad, mole at home'; 'king of a molehill'; and 'making mountains out of molehills.'

Leonard Woolf's autobiography entitled *Sowing* contains the following literary mole-lore: 'Lytton nicknamed him (E. M. Forster) the Taupe, partly because of his faint physical resemblance to a mole, but principally because he seemed intellectually and emotionally to travel underground, and every now and again pop up unexpectedly with some subtle observation or delicate quip which somehow or other he had found in the depths of the earth or of his own soul.'

Our fashionable new metaphor of mole as a labyrinthine and secret 'sleeper' burrowing away inside the Establishment has a certain seedy glamour for Brits, who are obsessed with spy stories, a genre in which they lead the world both in fiction and in non-fiction. Moles themselves might consider it an improvement on the previous proverbial and literary image of the mole as merely a half-blind, worm-snuffling, king-killing, idol-worshipping ravisher of lawns.

Le Carré himself, the mole-maker, gives a precise date and definition for the metaphor of mole as spy who builds a legitimate cover over a period of years by not engaging in spying activities until he is tapped for an important mission. The date when 'mole' first impinged on the British consciousness was 1976. Le Carré's definition: 'A mole is, I think, a genuine KGB term for somebody who burrows into the fabric of a bourgeois society and undermines it from within—somebody of the Philby sort who is recruited at a very tender age. There are people about whom, at a certain time, you guess the pattern of their ideological development, if you're a talent spotter working for the Russian Secret Service; and you winkle them into a corner and say: "We appreciate your feelings about this, but just keep very quiet—sooner or later we will need you, and when we do we will tell you."'

Well said, old mole! Canst work i' the Foreign Office so fast? What with the British passion for spies, and the other British passion for comfortable old clichés, I am afraid that Mr Mole is going to have to resign himself to the extension of his name.

When people called Howard become snobbish about their ancient name, as some of the sillier ones do, the way to take them down a peg is to remind them that their name is derived from Hog-ward, or pig-keeper. This is not strictly true, since, on the rare occasions when Howard was an occupational name, the Hog was a sheep, and Howard was a ewe-herd. But it generally shuts them up.

As for Messrs Mole, Eliza Cook, the pious Victorian poetastress, whose verse, according to her biographer, appealed very strongly to the middle classes, shall have the last word. It comes from her epic, *There is Nothing in Vain*:

'There's a mission, no doubt, for the mole in the dust,
　As there is for the charger, with nostrils of pride;
The sloth and the newt have their places of trust,
　And the *agents* are needed, for God has supplied.'

I fear, Mr A. J. Mole and others, you appear to be stuck with it. Just be grateful you are not named Sloth or Newt.

19/ NEW PROVERBS

Pleasures from the Book of Proverbs

One man's wit, and all men's wisdom.
Lord John Russell

Packs of grouse in the heather mean terrible weather. If a man wants to marry, he needs a card for Cash and Carry. When swallows be leaving, then lassies be conceiving. Perhaps you think, with Prince Hamlet, that the proverb is something musty. And it is true that they have been collecting proverbs since long before Solomon was King. ('There is no new thing under the sunne,' sayeth Ecclesiastes.) Proverbs are out of fashion, except in the remote parts of rural Britain.

We city sophisticates tend to look down on them as clichés and homely conventional wisdom. Also, so many proverbs seem to contradict each other. Too many cooks spoil the broth. But, on the other hand, many hands make light work. But proverbs are still part of the bedrock of the English language. Throughout the Middle Ages and until the eighteenth century proverbs were regarded as universal truths, and wheeled out to confirm or refute an argument.

Note how many proverbs were brought into currency by that marvellous scholar of the New Learning, Erasmus, in his *Adages*, including the original version, a rolling stone does not gather seaweed; so much more vivid, don't you think, than moss, with the image of a stone rolled back and forward by the tides for all eternity. Long lists of proverbs were compiled for the use of scholars in debate, parsons in the pulpit, and the leader-writing classes in their hasty lucubrations.

The proverb-making instinct is not wholly dead today, although proverbs have been partly superseded by catch-phrases, newspaper headlines, advertising jingles, and quotations from the famous. In 1982 the Oxford University Press published its *Concise Dictionary of Proverbs*, edited by J. A. Simpson, and corralled and branded all the new proverbs in common use in Britain in the twentieth century. It was fascinating to see systematically displayed how our brave new technologies are replacing classical maxims and the folk-lore of farming folk as sources of proverbs. Here is an example from computer technology, that prolific source of new jargon: 'Garbage in, garbage out.' In the mystery of data processing, garbage is the slang for incorrect output. This pretty proverb means that if you put rubbish into a computer, you will get rubbish out, a truth of which those of us who wrestle daily with the new technology are painfully aware. It is sometimes abbreviated to its acronymic form, GIGO.

By selecting your data, you can make statistics sing any song you want. 'Garbage in, garbage out' is a modern version of 'You can't make a silk purse out of a sow's ear.'

There are the various modern 'laws', including Parkinson's and Murphy's, 'if anything can go wrong, it will.' The latter is said to have been invented by George Nichols in 1949. Nichols was then a project manager working in California for the American firm of Northrop, and developed the maxim from a remark made by a colleague, Captain E. Murphy, of the Wright Field-Aircraft Laboratory. The contexts of the early quotations support this explanation. For instance, from *Aviation Mechanics Bulletin* 1955: 'Murphy's Law: If an aircraft part can be installed incorrectly, someone will install it that way.' This law is known more succinctly to *The Guardian* as Sod's Law. But its exemplary variant, 'The bread never falls but on its buttered side,' is older than Murphy. It can be traced back to A. D. Richardson's *Beyond Mississippi*, published in 1867: '*His* bread never fell on the buttered side.'

Many of the new proverbs come from across the Atlantic. 'The best things in life are free' was originally a line from a popular song. But are we quite sure that W. C. Fields was the onlie begetter of 'Never give a sucker an even break'? The legend is that he used it in the musical comedy *Poppy* (1923), though it does not occur in the libretto. Fields certainly made it his own and popularized it. But there is evidence that some anonymous poet of the peasantry thought of it first. Similarly, I thought that Harry Truman was the originator of the splendid proverb, 'If you don't like the heat, get out of the kitchen,' which he gave as a homely (in the British sense, homey in the American) reason for his retirement. It appears that in fact he cribbed the expression from his military jester, Major

General Harry Vaughan, who no doubt picked it up from somewhere in his childhood. Proverbs should have no authors. They are vernacular verse, Anon.

Only very rarely can we pin down the precise moment of a proverb's creation. But we can in the case of, 'The opera ain't over till the fat lady sings', which is my favourite modern proverb, to be dragged in at every opportunity. We know the exact moment of that one's birth from the *Washington Post* of 1978: 'One day, three years ago, Ralph Carpenter, who was then Texas Tech's sports information director, declared to the press box contingent in Austin, "The rodeo ain't over till the bull riders ride." Stirred to the top by that deep insight, San Antonio sports editor Dan Cook countered with, "The opera ain't over till the fat lady sings."'

Many of the new proverbs that we are coining today are agreeably hard-bitten as well as humorous. 'There's no such thing as a free lunch' was a colloquial axiom in United States economics of the Friedman school before it passed into general use. 'If you can't beat them, join them' seems to have been a political adage in the States, where 'beat' is usually replaced by 'lick'. There is Raymond Chandler's wonderfully world-weary shrug, 'You can't win them all.' Its variant, 'You win a few, you lose a few' has older roots. This useful expression of consolation or resignation must be of American origin, but its earliest citation is in Kipling's *Captains Courageous*: 'Thirty million dollars' worth of mistake, wasn't it? I'd risk it for that.' 'I lost some, and I gained some.'

Free collective bargaining, showing real popular roots, has come up with the majestic, 'If you pay peanuts, you get monkeys.' The earliest citation for that so far uncovered was in 1966. However, 'Unity is strength' goes back farther than King Arthur Scargill or King Lud to Homer, *Iliad* XIII, 237: 'Even weak men have strength in unity.'

Pace the pace of modern life, the proverb still lives. It counsels, warns, or consoles us in its folksy fashion. In spite of the proliferating and bewildering sources of advice from the media, we still have room for the homely-homey wisdom of our illiterate forefathers. The twentieth-century proverb, especially, counsels us, out of the side of the mouth like Bogart, to grin and bear it.

So, never choose your women or your linen by candlelight. Horses for courses. There's many a good tune played on an old fiddle. Proverbs are the poetry of the people. The opera ain't over till the fat lady sings.

20/ OSCAR

What's in a name?

> I agree with you entirely in condemning the mania of giving names to objects of any kind after persons still living. Death alone can seal the title of any man to this honor, by putting it out of his power to forfeit it.
> Thomas Jefferson, letter to Benjamin Rush, 1800

One of the harmless forms of immortality is as an eponym, by getting one's name into the dictionary as the father or mother of an eponymous word. As Jefferson remarked, the best eponyms are dead. The closest that I ever got to a living eponym was Oscar. He was a former colleague with a bullying manner and responsibilities for design and lay-out: the way that the words are presented on the page of a newspaper to make them look appetizing or sexy, as we (well, some of us) say in the inky trade. Oscar had a morbid passion for small pictures of people's heads across a single column; or mug-shots. On poor quality newsprint such pictures generally look like cow-pats. But Oscar thought that they diversified the page, giving it a waterfall effect, by which the eye cascaded down the page from small spotty picture to small spotty picture, skipping the boring old prose, like a man going over Niagara Falls in a barrel.

To this day in the Books Page of *The Times*, when a review falls ten centimetres short (the opposite of what book reviews generally do, alas), the Literary Editor says: 'I am just nipping across to the Picture Library to find an Oscar of Ronald Reagan', or, as it might be, Harold Macmillan, or Genghis Khan. There's glory for you! It remains to be seen whether this local eponymous word will catch on generally in the lexicon of the language.

The more famous Oscar, the androgynous gold-plated statuettes that film stars give each other in an orgy of mawkish self-congratulation, became an eponymous word in an equally haphazard way. The awards were introduced by Hollywood in 1927, and remained nameless for four years. Then Mrs Margaret Herrick, later to become secretary of the Motion Picture Academy, saw one, and observed that 'it reminds me of my Uncle Oscar.' A newspaper columnist, even shorter of copy than movie-hackettes usually are, overheard her and publicized the name: 'Employees have affectionately dubbed their famous statuette "Oscar".' It has become part of the language.

Mrs Herrick's uncle was, in fact, her second cousin, Oscar Pierce, son of a rich western pioneer family, who had formerly lived in Texas. Mr Pierce's main concerns were growing wheat and fruit, and making money. It is not recorded whether he was interested in the cinema.

The study of eponyms is full of ingenious answers to puzzling questions. Whose name was Mudd? He was the ill-informed and dozy country doctor who treated John Wilkes Booth, the murderer of Abraham Lincoln, without realizing who he was or what he had done. The authorities did not believe in Mudd's plea of ignorance and innocence, convicted him on a charge of conspiracy, and sentenced him to life imprisonment. The wretched Mudd lived out his life in jail, and it became fashionable to associate his name with anything connected with the assassination. Mudd was officially pardoned in 1869 by President Andrew Johnson, but his name is still mud.

Who went maverick first? He was Samuel A. Maverick (1803–70), a lawyer and signatory of the Texas Declaration of Independence. He became a cattle rancher after he had accepted a small herd in payment of a debt. Maverick branded these with his MK brand, but, having little time for his role as cattleman, he failed to brand their progeny. His neighbours started to refer to any unbranded stray stock as 'one of Maverick's'. Appropriation of an unbranded calf that was not following its mother was not classed as rustling. In the confusion of the Civil War there were more unbranded long-horn mavericks in Texas than branded stock. Not all of them belonged to Samuel Maverick, but he gave them his name.

Who was the first Nosey Parker? Dr Matthew Parker (1504–75), Archbishop of Canterbury, and notorious for his zeal in poking his nose into anything remotely concerned with church business. Who was the real McCoy? This question is so vexed that I doubt whether any of the answers offered is satisfactory. But the folk etymology I like best derives the eponymous word from the boxer Norman

Selby (1873–1940), who fought under the name of Kid McCoy. A drunk insisted on picking a quarrel with him, in spite of being warned that it was a mistake. Eventually McCoy lost his temper and laid him out. When he came round, the drunk shook his head and said: 'You're right; that was the real McCoy.' A charming etymology, but unpersuasive.

Who was the original lush? This is another disputed eponym. The slang term for a habitual drunkard is American, but its roots are said to be English. 'Lush' meaning strong beer is listed in Captain Francis Grose's *A Classical Dictionary of the Vulgar Tongue* (London, 1785); associated with it are 'to lush' meaning to booze, and 'lushey' meaning drunk. Grose gives as an example: 'The rolling kiddeys had a spree, and got bloody lushey.'

The name may be derived from Dr Thomas Lushington (1590–1661), a drinking clergyman who did his best drinking with Bishop Richard Corbet. The anecdote says that, whenever they met for a session, they would say to each other, 'Here's to thee, Corbet', and, 'Here's to thee, Lushington.' There was a drinking club called the City of Lushington associated with the Harp Tavern in Great Russell Street, London, and frequented by actors. The growth of eponyms is dark and doubtful, as well as delightful.

Another agreeable Snark of an eponym is the firm of Irish builders in Liverpool known as Jerry Brothers. In the early nineteenth century they are said to have made their names by putting up houses of showy but shoddy material. The houses fell down, and the Jerry Brothers gave their name to jerry-built. The etymology is unsupported by any documentation, and therefore, I regret, itself jerry-built. The term is more likely to have come from Jericho, the walls of which fell down at the blast of Joshua's trumpets.

The authentic and undisputed queen of the eponym is Mademoiselle Antoinette de Poubelle, whose necessity was the mother of invention. Unable to leave the room during the unnaturally long sermons of Louis Bourdaloue, an interminable preacher of the court of Louis XIV, she hid in her muff a lidded vase, a long-sitting lady's comforter, which has ever since been known as a *poubelle* or *bourdalou*. So long as the wild boar delights in the mountain tops, the fish live in the rivers, and the bees feed on thyme, so long will the glory of her name remain.

The full specification of the *bourdalou* is worth recording: *'une vase de nuit de forme ovale et de petites dimensions, sur le fonds duquel était peint un oeil entouré de légendes grivoises.'*

86

Lovely as she is, I regret to say that Mme Antoinette de Poubelle is apocryphal, though Bourdaloue was real. The true, the blushful *poubelle* is a *récipient à couvercle pour les ordures ménagères*. It was invented, introduced, and named by Eugène René Poubelle (1831–1907), *Préfet de la Seine*. At the beginning of his term of office in 1884 he introduced the *poubelle,* a dustbin with a lid, to Paris. It is still emptied daily there. They order this matter better in France. That, at least, is my story; and I am sticking to it. The etymology of eponyms is a dark and delicate business.

21/ PRONUNCIATION

Silence is deep as eternity, speech is shallow as time

Write with the learned, pronounce with the vulgar.
Benjamin Franklin, *Poor Richard's Almanac*, 1738

A century ago there was something called received pronunciation or standard English. It was defined by the inventor of the name as 'a class dialect rather than any local dialect—the language of the educated all over Britain.' In living memory middle-class parents in the home counties around London anxiously drilled their darling children to pronounce long 'o' to rhyme with 'low' rather than 'cow', so that they should not sound like the village children.

But even then opinions were sharply divided about the merits of what was popularly called the Oxford accent. Some admired it as the best kind of English spoken by the best, or at any rate the best-educated, people. Others attacked it as snobbish, slovenly, affected, and the dialect of an effete social clique.

Today, with such diverse groups of people pronouncing their own dialects of English all over the world, the notion of a single correct English pronunciation is nonsense. The engaging sing-song of Bombay-speak *is* correct for those who chatter it along the Victoria Garden Road. An Oxford accent, though acceptable in much of the English-speaking world, is grotesque and even unintelligible in parts of Glasgow and Watts County, Los Angeles. It is a matter as much of intelligibility as of class or race rancour.

Pronunciation is changing fast. It always has changed faster than other elements of the language. One factor of change is the dominance of American influence, so that Englishmen now put the stress on the first syllable of words like 'research' and 'defect', instead of putting all the emphasis on the second syllable with a hardly perceptible vowel sound in the first.

A second factor of change is the complete victory of the speak-as-you-spell movement. A generation ago, when standard English pronunciation was the property of an élite educated at the public schools and the older universities, the way we spoke was a minefield of conventional pronunciations to hoist the unwary and the uneducated sky-high. We pronounced 'girl' as 'gairl' or 'gel', and took pains not to aspirate such words as 'hotel' and 'humour'. We said 'rejment' for regiment and 'medsin' for medicine. These tricky pronunciations were in-jokes and class indicators, especially with upper class proper names such as Marjoribanks, pronounced Marchbanks, and Cholmondeley, pronounced Chumli. Today, now that pronunciation has been democratized, there is a strong tendency to pronounce as we spell, to say 'golf' rather than 'guff', to say 'extraordinary' with six syllables rather than three.

A third factor of change is a chauvinist distaste for supposedly pretentious foreign pronunciations. We bluff John Bulls now firmly Anglicize our pronunciation of fancy froggy words taken from the French such as *cadre* or *femme fatale*. Garridge me no garahges in these populist times. Working against this tendency is a curious little countertendency to pronounce the names of foreign places as the natives do. I suspect that this may derive from the arrival of mass foreign travel. At any rate it is a sport as well as a pain to hear a television news reader conscientiously trying to get her tongue around Valencia or Firenze as the natives do it. Previous generations gave themselves no trouble with Florence, which has been established in English language and pronunciation since the fourteenth century.

Another factor influencing the rapid change in pronunciation is the decision by the television and radio, particularly the most influential BBC, to open its broadcasts to accents that would have been called, in the days of received pronunciation, 'uneducated'. This was obviously the right decision. To restrict broadcasting on the mass media to a small élite selected by the Shibboleth of a class accent would have been as silly as selecting only red-heads to read the news, or Gideon picking his army by the way they drank when they came to a river. It is significant that the BBC still uses Oxford accents to broadcast on its overseas services, because foreigners not to the manner born need some regular standard of pronunciation to understand what is being said.

All these changes upset people who had it drummed into them

at old-fashioned grammar schools that there was a single correct form of English, and a standard of proper English pronunciation. They tend to write to *The Times* complaining that standards are slipping, that the BBC is corrupting the Queen's English, and that the troops of Midian prowl and prowl around, threatening even the way we speak. This may be bully for *The Times*, but sometimes I wish that they would direct their complaints to the supposed offender.

The first thing to say to them is that pronunciation is changing all the time in a living language. The golden age when English was spoken correctly never existed; though many of those who complain misapprehend that it came close to perfection in the days when they were being taught it in an old-fashioned prescriptive way. If Chaucer were brought back to us on pilgrimage on a time-palfrey, we should not understand much of what he was saying. Shakespeare and Queen Elizabeth I would sound to us like stage yokels speaking Mummerset.

People who are agitated by changes in pronunciation are vexed by the change in stress from the first syllable to the second of a word like 'formidable': the reverse of the phenomenon that Fowler described as the recessive accent. 'Formidable', with the accent on '-mid-' sounds to them untraditional, unetymological, ugly, and *wrong*. But such stresses do shift all the time, backwards as Fowler observed, and forwards. 'Comméndable' sounds right today with the stress on the second syllable '-mend-'. In Shakespeare's time the stress was evidently on the first syllable:

'Tis sweet and cómmendable in thy nature, Hamlet.'
    'Silence is only cómmendable
In a neat's tongue dried and a maid not vendible.'

There is no linguistic rule that English has to follow the pronunciation of languages we borrow words from, or we should say 'cohmic' with a long first syllable, and 'datta' with a short one. But classical quantities used to decide where the ictus or stress lay. Even that rule has gone, as was exemplified by the controversial production of *The Greeks* by the Royal Shakespeare Company in 1980. Until recently only a cad would have pronounced Athenagoras, with the ictus on the penultimate syllable, or Lysistrata to rhyme with 'Miss Potato'. But the Shakespeareans did. The 'incorrect' new stress on the second syllable of Uranus sounds rudely anal. At least it is easier to say than the classical pronunciation.

Class, as well as education and convention, affects pronunciation. But these new pronunciations are not just a matter of U and non-U.

English protestants say reféctory, and Catholics réfectory. In Ulster Ian Paisley says Lúndundry, but Gerry Fitt (if he can bring himself to pronounce the name in full) says Londondérry. Freudians are ambívalent, and Jungians ambiválent. Moderates speak of cápitalism, and extremists of capítalism, which sounds uglier, with a spit on the second syllable. It might help industrial relations if the Confederation of British Industry and the Trades Union Congress could agree on where the stress comes in a 'dispute'.

As far as a rule can be worked out for such a gloriously free and do-it-yourself language as English, it used to be customary to put the stress on principal words such as nouns and verbs, not on subsidiary words such as adjectives and prepositions, except for special emphasis. Even this rule is being changed by the broadcasters, vexing their listeners more than anything else they mispronounce.

It has become a trick of television reporters and news readers to put the stress plonkingly on their prepositions: the PRIME Minister held a meeting OF the Cabinet yesterday TO discuss the future OF the Government's linguistic legislation. They sound like one-legged drunks hopping from lamp-post to lamp-post. Why they do it is a mystery. To lend an air of urgency to an otherwise boring and unconvincing narrative? To give themselves time to read the idiot-guide of the teleprompter? To sound trendy?

There is little point in saying they are wrong. But we can say that it sounds ugly, and resolve not to do it ourselves until perhaps it eventually becomes standard English pronunciation.

22/ RIGHT

Let's get this right

> Be sure you are right: then go ahead.
> David Crockett's motto in the War of 1812

Where do the terms left and right as politicial labels come from, pray? Oh, come on, Philip: every schoolboy knows that. Kindly leave the page. It is generally accepted that the leftness and rightness of politics originated in the French National Assembly of 1789. The reactionaries sat on the right, the moderates in the centre, and the democrats and extremists on the left. This established the custom that in many legislatures the radicals sit on the left-hand side, as seen from the chair. At Westminster, and in most assemblies of the Commonwealth, the government sits on the right, and the opposition on the left.

It was all recorded by our most dramatic historian: 'There is a Right Side (*Côté Droit*), a Left Side (*Côté Gauche*); sitting on M. Le Président's right hand, or on his left; the *Côté Droit* conservative; the *Côté Gauche* destructive. Intermediate is Anglomaniac Constitutionalism, or Two-Chamber Royalism; with its Mouniers, its Lallys —fast verging towards nonentity.' Thank you, Thomas. Nicely put, in instantly identifiable style.

This geographical arrangement did not emerge out of thin air during the world earthquake of the Revolution. It was derived from *les États généraux*, which met intermittently under the French monarchy from 1302 to 1789, when they were reconstituted as the National Assembly. When the Estates-General met, the First and Second Estates (clergy and nobles) were seated to the right of the king, and the relatively radical Third Estate (the bourgeoisie) perforce to his left. This precedence reflected the very ancient prejudice that the right-hand side is more honourable; cf. the use of 'sinister', derived from the Latin for 'left.'

92

That is the authorized version. In that case, why does Menenius Agrippa, nearly two millennia before the French Revolution, refer to the conservative party as the right? You remember: brave old patrician, devoted friend of Coriolanus, parable of the Belly and its Members, 'this man was my beloved in Rome.' In *Coriolanus*, Act II, Scene 1, line about 20, I make it in my edition, Menenius Agrippa addresses the two Tribunes of the People: 'This is strange now. Do you know how you are censured here in the city—I mean of us o' th' right-hand file? Do you?' What is all this about Romans, even if they are Jacobean Romans, using right as a label for the conservatives? It turns received opinion on the subject on its head. Rum, not to say mysterious, *hein*?

When the matter was first raised, I took it that the Roman Senate must have been arranged with patricians to the right, and plebeian senators *conscripti* to the left; that the French National Assembly, which consciously took many models from the Roman Republic, copied it in this too; and that the Roman origin of the right and left arrangement had eluded commentators and exegetes. The trouble is that I can find no evidence in the sources, and nor can anybody else. We know that the Senate used to meet in various places that had to be both public and consecrated. We know that sittings were private, but with opened doors. We know that the tribunes of the plebs had to sit in the vestibule before they were let in. We know that procedure changed over a dozen centuries until the Roman Senate faded from the records in AD 603.

There is some evidence that the senators did *not* sit in party groupings. Cicero, addressing Catiline: 'And then again, when you arrived inside the Senate, every seat anywhere near your own was promptly vacated. As soon as you took your place, all the former consuls, whom you have repeatedly marked down for assassination, left that entire area of seats unoccupied and empty.' That suggests, does it not, that Catiline was sitting among his opponents, not with his mates of the Militant Demagogic Tendency. But if the Roman Senate did not divide left and right, where in the world did Menenius Agrippa get his notion about the right-hand file? I think we should be told.

One could pursue this Roman red herring farther into other assemblies such as the Comitia curiata, the Comitia plebis tributa, and, preferably, the Comitia centuriata, which was usually assembled on the Campus Martius in military order, sc. in order of the military equipment that the classes could afford, with those who could

93

provide the panoply necessary to be a member of the Equites to the right. But one would be wasting one's time and one's readers' patience. However, the point about military order gives the clue.

The right-hand file is a military not a political metaphor. Agrippa's remark does not appear to refer to the position in which senators sat, to which no reference is made in Plutarch's *Coriolanus*, which was, of course, Shakespeare's authority, in North's translation. Agrippa is referring to himself not as a senator, but as an old soldier bowed down with medals and pig-headedness. He is alluding—albeit anachronistically—to the sixteenth-century custom of placing the choicest men in the right-hand files of the company in order to honour them. To take the right-hand file was a military metaphor meaning 'to take precedence.' Compare and contrast Philip Massinger's *The Picture, a tragi-comedy* (1629), III, 5: 'There are Many who may take the right-hand file of you.'

Come to that, I am not sure than Menenius Agrippa was being anachronistic after all. We can trace the custom of placing one's bravest men in the place of honour on the right of the line back to the hoplite armies of ancient Greece, where each man relied on his right-hand neighbour for protection, because his own shield, on his left arm, could not adequately cover his right side. A famous consequence of this order of battle, attested in Thucydides and elsewhere, was the tendency of the man on the extreme right of the line to edge farther to his right in order to outflank the enemy and protect his vulnerable side from the spears and arrows of outrageous Spartans.

For that matter, we do not have to be content with secular authorities for the superiority of the right-hand file. We can go to Holy Writ. *Psalm CX*, 1: 'The Lord said unto my Lord, Sit thou at my right hand, until I make thine enemies thy footstool.' *Ecclesiastes* X, 2: 'A wise man's heart is at his right hand; but a fool's heart at his left.' 'At thy right hand there are pleasures for evermore', says the Psalmist (XVI, 11), and we perpetuate his prescription in the placing of guests at formal dinner-tables to this day. The most authoritative statement of the left and right division is given in *Matthew* XXV, 33, about the Son of man coming back in glory: 'And he shall set the sheep on his right hand, but the goats on the left.'

Shakespeare was in the first generation of Englishmen fully exposed to compulsory attendance at church on Sunday, introduced by Henry VIII, and divine service in the vernacular, introduced by

Edward VI. From childhood he was indoctrinated by a vernacular catechism and Cranmer's translation of the creeds, stating that Jesus Christ, His only Son, Our Lord, 'sitteth' or 'is seated' on the right hand of God the Father Almighty. We might also speculate about the relative positions of bride, bridegroom, and bride's father at a wedding before and after the knot is tied, as viewed by themselves and the priest; likewise the separation of the seating of their respective families.

There is a very ancient tradition, preceding the French Revolution, Shakespeare's Menenius Agrippa, and Menenius Agrippa himself, of seating the good on the right, and the not-so-good or downright bad on the left. We can draw the agreeable political inference that the Establishment, or those with power to control the written word (or seating arrangements) are by nature conservative, and accordingly equate good and the right with conservatism.

23/ SIC

Giving Classic offence to Latin lovers

The Romans would never have found time to conquer the world if they had been obliged first to learn Latin.
Heinrich Heine, Reisebilder, II, 1826

Latin quotation may be the parole of the educated class. It once was, but no longer. As the revolting peasants with Jack Cade shout in the second part of *Henry VI*: 'Away with him, away with him! he speaks Latin.' Today Latin quotation may be a way of showing off, and therefore bad manners: it depends on your audience. But it can be a risky business.

I have this friend, an eminent physician, who likes to flaunt the considerable remnants, not entirely ruinous, of an old-fashioned classical education. He was dictating a letter into one of those beastly little cassette dictation machines, and wanted to chide me for some error or another of the sort that will happen in the best-regulated writing. In condonation he wanted to say that he had himself been guilty of the same error when younger. Accordingly he dictated, in parenthesis, '(*experto crede*)'.

His new secretary, not yet accustomed to his bad habits, and reluctant to admit that she could not confidently transcribe anything that he dictated, typed a letter including the phrase, '... (the expert O'Grady)'. So Latin quotation misheard has created out of thin air a new expert for our world already too full of experts. I take him to be a most distinguished though insubstantial Professor O'Grady, to whose expert authority all problems of grammar, idiom, scholarly taste, and forensic psychiatry are referred, and whose rulings I await and revere as though writ in tablets of the Blarney Stone.

96

A similar Latin misadventure befell Professor Geoffrey Elton when he was delivering (*ex tempore*, without a script) his inaugural lecture as Professor of English Constitutional History at Cambridge. For his peroration he thundered into Latin with the magnificent line from Lucan's Stoic epic, the *Bellum Civile: Victrix causa deis placuit, sed victa Catoni*; 'the winning side pleased the gods, but the losing one pleased Cato.' The stenographer taking it all down for the off-print of the inaugural, published by the Cambridge University Press, having reproduced a perfect transcript so far, recorded this sentence as: '*Victrix causa deis placuit*, said Victor Catoni.' Professor O'Grady, meet Victor Catoni.

Latin is dangerous, now that it is no longer essential knowledge for the educated. However, it would be cowardly and handicapping oneself to avoid all Latin tags and quotations in English on the grounds that one might be misunderstood. Some of them express meanings that cannot be expressed half so neatly and compendiously in Anglo-Saxon, e.g. *e.g.* itself, and *i.e.*, *sc.*, *viz.*, *mutatis mutandis*, *de gustibus non disputandum*, *anno Domini*, and dozens, and I dare say one could make a case for hundreds, of others. Many of them, e.g. in English law, have become part of the English language as well as Latin. Some of them are being given different meanings in English from their original Latin meanings: e.g. *alibi*, and *alter ego*.

One little Latin word that we often misunderstand and abuse for polemical purposes in journalism is *sic*. As every schoolboy and girl used to know, it means 'so'. Its idiomatic use in the word-box of English grammar is in brackets (*sic*) after some quote word or phrase, to confirm that it is an accurate quotation, or gives the writer's deliberate meaning, rather than a typographical error, or editor's emendation.

I am afraid, human nature being what it is, *sic* is usually employed to point triumphantly at a solecism or controversial point in the quotation, to make it clear that the writer is a superior person of impeccable linguistic manners, and to distance him or her from the booby being quoted. *Exempli gratia*, 'The President said that his (or her) views were very different than (*sic*) the Inspector's.' That is a silly and frivolous use of *sic*. The quoter means: 'Observe by the way the President's ignorance of correct grammar. He may think that "different" takes "than", but I know better.' It would be simpler and less Smart-Alecky to amend the sentence to 'different from' or 'different to' (*sic*). That last *sic* means: 'Please do not write triumphantly to assert that "different" can take only "from", and that "to" is a solecism. Both prepositions are found in the best authors and are equally idiomatic.' There's a nice long knock-down argument for you crammed into the tiny Latin word. It might even be simpler to accept the convenient and spreading American idiom that 'different' can indeed take 'than'.

Sic can be abused for a political as well as a grammatical sneer. 'The Palestinian (or Israeli) delegation appealed for funds from the public to continue their work of enlightening (*sic*) the world about the justice of their cause.' That *sic* says: 'What cheek! How dare such zealous and unscrupulous propagandists claim that what they are up to is enlightenment?' Since nobody can doubt that 'enlightening' is an authentic quotation, the correct way to draw attention to it, and distance the writer from the claim, is not (*sic*), but to quarantine the word inside inverted commas.

A more sensible use of (*sic*) is to mean: 'Yes, I do mean that, in spite of your natural doubts.' E.g., 'The Minister said that we should have to settle on a definite date such as 1987 or 1989 (*sic*).' The useful little (*sic*) is inserted in case you were worried about what had happened to 1988.

Another sensible use of (*sic*) is to say: 'Yes, this is an accurate quotation, not a misprint; do not write to complain.' E.g., 'Referring to the Honours List, the Leader of the Opposition remarked, "Quiz *custodiet ipsos custodes*?" (*sic*).' We have not misprinted *Quiz* for *quis*. The Leader of the Opposition was referring wittily to the remarkable ennoblement of quiz-masters and other second-rate television personalities.

But the polemical and erroneous (*sic*) use of (*sic*) is as a concise sneer or method of emphasizing the preceding words, either for praise, or more usually for blame. For example: 'The President appealed to all men and women of good will, irrespective of race, or creed, or political party (*sic*), to pull together for the sake of the great society.' That (*sic*) says: 'Look who's appealing for national unity above party divisions! That old party hack never drew a breath or lifted a finger without a political motive.'

'The Secretary General of the Trade Union said that without more money on the table his members would continue to work to rule (*sic*).' That little (*sic*) means: 'We all know that working to rule means doing as little as possible and being generally bloody-minded and obstructive, while continuing to draw their excessive wages.'

98

That is not what the useful little Latin word is for (*sic*). However, I dare say that we journalists and other controversialists are going to continue to abuse the handy little stiletto with the blood-thirstiness of medieval Florentines.

24/ SLANG

Waiting for the red letter day

> Slang is the speech of him who robs the literary garbage carts on their way to the dumps.
> Ambrose Bierce, *Collected Works*, VIII

New slang flows into the language all the time, enlivening it and stirring it up, as the Rhône flows into Lac Léman between Villeneuve and St Gingolph. Old slang does not flow away so fast. It takes some of the water centuries to pass through Lac Léman and exit at Geneva by Rhône Part II. Anybody who has ever been swimming beside the Château de Chillon (a thousand feet in depth below, its massy waters meet and flow, I suppose, but they flow exceeding slow) may well suspect that some of the water has been hanging around there since Hannibal passed by.

How much longer, do you suppose, are we going to carry on using 'in the red' as a colloquialism to describe one's, unhappily natural, state of having taken out more money than one has in the bank, now that computerized bank statements are printed all in the black? As the old proverb recommends, speak not of my debts, unless you mean to pay them.

The pawky computer at the Royal Bank of Scotland puts DR after the alarming figure that one's account is overdrawn, to indicate that it would have used red ink, if computers could. Common computers of lesser banks apparently put OD, which, to ageing or aghast eyes, can look bewilderingly like the percentage symbol, %.

'In the red' has flowed into the great, gaudy lake of English slang only recently. The earliest example that the diligent hunters of the *OED Supplement* have been able to track down comes from a *Wise-*

Crack Dictionary published in 1926: '*In the red*, losing money in show parlance.' The fact that it needed explanation suggests that the phrase was then a newcomer. It caught on, literally, to mean being overdrawn, in debt, and losing money; and figuratively. I have a cutting from *The Times* about two batsmen (cricket, Wilbur, cricket) opening Somerset's second innings with commendable vigour, so that Leicestershire 'went further into the red.' You can get into the red with runs, as well as pounds or dollars.

'Out of the red' came into the language at about the same time. *Publisher's Weekly* of 1928: 'About 966 copies more and the title will be out of the red.' According to the sage Partridge, 'in the red's' much less used complement, 'in the black', a consummation devoutly to be wish'd, but rarely achieved, hardly antecedes 1945. He was wrong about that, at any rate as far as the United States was concerned. The *OED* found a citation from the *New York Times* of 1928: '*In the black*, showing a profit.'

What is odd is that the colourful idiom flourishes, even though the practice to which it refers is obsolete. But then red-letter day also survives, even though the custom of printing saints' days in red ink on almanacs and weekly orders of service of the Church of England no longer impinges on the national consciousness. Some calendars have adapted the old practice by printing public holidays and weekends in red. Slang lingers on in the national vocabulary long after its original point is forgotten, in the same way that the water sticks around the Château de Chillon long after it should have flowed on towards the sea.

'In the red' is a surprisingly longevous meaningless idiom. Presumably it will carry on until generations who have never known red ink on a bank balance take over the language. We are conservative as well as innovative with our language. 'Under tow' has undergone a rather different metamorphosis. It is a modern distortion of an old idiom. It is becoming idiomatic, in all but the specialized nautical publications, to speak of a vessel being under tow.

An undertow is a peril to bathers that lurks off certain beaches, the seaward undercurrent that follows the breaking of a wave on the beach. The correct nautical idiom, from the Elizabethan seamen who introduced it to David Livingstone ('We took the hippopotamus in tow', and rather him than me) and until today among seamen is 'in tow'. A possible distinction, which has not yet established itself, is that the towing ship has the towed ship in tow; the towed ship

101

is under tow. But the 'under tow' idiom is comparatively recent, and sounds wet.

I suspect that analogy, that potent force in changing language, has been at work with 'under tow'. There is a small group of idioms that refer to the progress of a vessel through the water: under oars, under sail, under her own steam, and under weigh. I think that, now that we are a nation of motorists in traffic jams on motorways, instead of a nation of seafarers, we have altered the idiom to 'under tow' by analogy with these other idioms. For their nasty purposes motorists and other rude mechanics have recently invented the idiom 'on tow'. It will be interesting to see which idiom wins.

Another nasty new press idiom is 'horse-riding', with its even more tautological 'horse-back-riding.' May we not assume that any riding reported in the press will, unless otherwise specified, be upon a horse? And, for that matter, upon the horse's back rather than some other part of its body. Cossacks are said to have a penchant for passing under their horses' bellies while at full gallop. But even the most restless Cossack appears to spend most of his mounted time in the general area between the animal's withers and its crupper. John Betjeman satirized horse-back-riding in a competition to cram the greatest number of solecisms into the shortest space with, I regret to tell you, the lines:

> 'And Howard's out riding on horse-back
> so do come and take some with me.'

The invitation was to tea.

Metaphors and clichés grow old like slang. We use them without noticing what we are saying, without a ripple passing through our minds. So we end up saying strange things.

For example, it has become common to talk of locking the stable door after the horse has bolted. This is odd, and suggests that our generation is not at home with horses. Horses are silly creatures, but even they seldom if ever bolt from their stables. Stable is home, where they eat and sleep and are happy, and do not have to stagger about bow-legged carrying members of the horsy class. At the end of a journey, when they realize that they are coming near to home, they tend to bolt *towards* the stable.

The proverb is very old, goes back to the days of horse thieves, and should be to bolt the stable door after the horse has been stolen. It is too late to shut the stable door when the steed has been stolen. There is a (doggy) Latin source from the twelfth century:

Maxima pars pecore amisso praesepia claudit.

Most people close the fold after the sheep have gone missing. In English in the fourteenth century Gower wrote in *Confessio Amantis*: 'For when the great steed is stole, then he taketh heed, and maketh the stable door fast.'

Today we are less familiar with horse thieves. Bolting is the sort of irrational act we expect from horses. Accordingly we have transferred the bolt from the beginning to the end of the sentence, from the stable door to the horse. And so our modern variant makes nonsense of the old proverb.

Turning to a different kettle of fish, over the past generation we have created a nonsensical proverb about a different kettle of fish. Different from what, pray? It would be disturbing enough to have one kettle of fish. To have a different one as well would be too much.

The proverbial expression is, correctly, a pretty or fine kettle of fish, meaning a muddle, snafu, or awkward state of things. 'Here's a pretty kettle of fish,' wrote Gilbert, that precise user of English. 'Here's a pretty kettle of fish,' also cried Mrs Towwouse in Fielding's *Joseph Andrews* (1742). 'If so, we shall have a fine kettle of fish at Seringapatam,' wrote the Duke of Wellington in 1800. There is indeed a shortage of metaphors for difference, since the old horse of a different colour is now archaic. There are those who say, 'a different pair of shoes.' The painter William Nicholson used to say, 'a different pair of socks.' But what possible sense of difference does a kettle of fish signify? Yet the extraordinary metaphor has been adopted by our best writers. Evelyn Waugh in *Put Out More Flags*: 'Until now the word "Colonel" for Basil had connoted an elderly rock-gardener on Barbara's G.P.O list. This formidable man of his own age was another kettle of fish.' And J. L. Austin, of all people, that exquisitely precise linguistic philosopher: 'Looking at a distant village on a very clear day across a valley, is a very different kettle of fish from seeing a ghost.' Some fish!

A more recent metaphor that seems to be straying is the one about mending fences. It is coming along nicely as a Janus expression, *sc.* one that looks in two directions at once, and has two opposing meanings. Half the people who use it think it means something like 'look to your moat', and defend your home base against the troops of Midian. The other half think it means something like 'building bridges', and re-establishing good relations with one's neighbours. Congressmen go home from Washington to mend their fences, renew contacts with, make their peace with, and generally butter up their constituents.

The latter meaning seems to be winning. Since the English language is a democracy, there is little point in arguing about who is right. But it is instructive to consider how the phrase and the confusion arose.

Webster supports the idea of mending fences as a defensive act against the enemy: 'To improve or strengthen or consolidate (one's position) by negotiation, manoeuvring, similar activity.' We could derive the metaphor from the range wars in the United States in the last century, familiar to those of us who enjoy westerns. Smallholders enclose their land with barbed-wire fences to keep the cattle out. Cattle barons led by Spencer Tracy in a black hat ride up and pull out fences. Smallholders mend fences and defy cattle-owners. Good little guys win in the end.

The alternative, irenic sense of mending fences comes from the agricultural truth that good fences make good neighbours. If the wire sags or the stones fall in your fence (a melancholy attribute of fences that I have helped to erect), your Blackface sheep will be through the gap, eating your neighbour's grass, and your tups impregnating his pedigree gimmers, before you can say Jack Hermes, patron of sheep-stealers. Good neighbours agree to mend their march fences together. Bad neighbours are always quarreling about fences.

A factor in the confusion is that the phrase 'Good fences make good neighbours' is connected with Robert Frost's poem *Mending Wall*, probably the most popular of his works in the United States. The repeated phrase that closes the poem is, 'Good fences make good neighbours.' Frost uses the British spelling in the last word. Counter to this phrase is the repeated line, 'Something there is that doesn't love a wall,' which is stating the reaction of nature to the territorial rights felt by man. 'Good fences make good neighbours' sounds like a proverb. It seems to me to indicate neither that relations with the neighbo(u)rs are bad, nor that they are good; it is simply a bull-headed New England rationalization of isolation (personal maybe; national, perhaps).

In his later years Frost unwittingly became the kind of self-caricature that most endears old men to wide audiences; and he always closed his public readings with this poem. Out of the fuzzy welter of affection for the old man, audiences gradually came to assume that the closing line meant that good neighbours inevitably had good fences, and that it was therefore a way of repairing

104

damaged relations if one put one's fences in good order. In fact, in the poem the statement is rather a curmudgeonly one; perhaps in the context even unnatural.

So there you are. You pays your money, and you takes your choice. Myself, I shall take care to avoid the phrase.

25/ SPORT

Getting a kick out of games

> When the rules of the game prove unsuitable for victory, the gentlemen of England change the rules of the game.
> Harold Laski, address to the Communist Academy, Moscow, July 1934

All games are silly. But then, so are human beings. The thing to do with sports and games is to play them, having first made up your mind whether you are going to play like an English Gentleman (or a Cheltenham Lady), or to win. Failing that, next best is to watch them from the Shed, or the Mound, or the Hill, or the Pavilion, or whatever other name the local sportsmen call their enclosure. After that, at three removes from reality, you can read about them in the papers, or listen to commentaries on them on the radio or television. After that, you can do the Pools. It is significant for the British understanding of sport that our principal newspaper for those who bet on horse-races is called *The Sporting Life*, and that those who like a flutter are referred to, at any rate by the bookmakers who live off them, as 'sportsmen'.

Most games are exciting to play (golf and Scrabble are exceptions: their attraction is that they are the apotheosis of boredom for the walking dead), interesting to watch, and really quite boring to read about; unless, of course, you have stylish and sprightly sporting scribes. One of the wonders of journalism is to see an old pro sporting hack, late at night, surrounded by the bedlam of the fans after the match has finished, dictating a thousand words of copy that will sound interesting and coherent in the cold light of day over breakfast on the following morning. Sporting journalism, because of the speed at which it is done, is a source of much solecism and vulgarity. It is also a source of lively new jargon and slang, because of the daily
106

intolerable wrestle to transfer the excitement of the stadium and the ring in a fresh way to the inky arena of the printed page.

You cannot go on saying that somebody kicked a ball, and somebody else kicked it back again; which is, in fact, a plain description of a football match. So that is why on the sports pages of the less literate papers footballs are rarely kicked, and even more rarely headed, but 'hammered', 'struck', 'knocked', 'stroked', 'guided', 'nodded', 'nudged', 'zapped', and even 'hit' into the net.

A recent trendy term for a team, imported, I suspect, from the United States, is a 'squad'. American football teams have different squads for different phases of the game, not just offense and defense, but even for such brief phases as taking kicks, so that a side's leading goal-kicker is on the field of play doing his stuff for only a few minutes in an entire season. This is democratic, because it enables almost anybody at an American College to make it into some seldom used squad in one of their football sides. The term is less suitable for British sports. Squad was originally applied, as an elegant variation, to Association Football. But squads now happen in the best-regulated teams of Rugby Football, cricket, athletics, and such traditional and energetic English sports as darts.

If used to make a nice distinction, the word adds something to the sporting lexicon. A squad ought to be a pool of players from which the team is to be selected. English football managers have squads of twenty or thirty players training together, from whom the final XI, about to be annihilated by Iceland Reserves, is chosen. If it is used, as 'squad' often is, merely as a synonym for a team or side, that is an example of inelegant variation and otiosity.

Here is an example of a recent fad in cricket jargon: Americans and others who are trained to think that cricket is incomprehensible as well as silly may skip this paragraph. For years we peacefully talked about batsmen receiving, getting, taking, or facing the bowling. Now the Colemanballs (named after David Coleman, one of our more exuberant sporting commentators on television) rage is to talk and write invariably about the batsmen 'taking strike'. There may be an influence from baseball here. It does not seem to me that much more striking a phrase. Like all sporting jargon, it may have only a short life. If it follows the usual pattern, it will be so over-used that it will become a laughing stock, and eventually die of shame, in the way that 'over the moon' and 'sick as a parrot' have become joke expressions for footballers to express delight and gloom, and in the way that our boxing scribes no longer write about

107

'tapping the claret' as a distasteful metaphor for making somebody's nose bleed.

Another trendy phrase in sporting slang describes runners who make a spurt as 'kicking'. You know the sort of thing: 'Howard is coming into the crown of the last bend now, and, MY GOD, he's KICKING ... look at him go ...', etc. ad nauseam and hysteriam. I assume that the kicking in question is imagined to be backwards like a horse, not forwards like a cow or sideways at the opposition. It still seems to me a funny metaphor for what one does when sprinting.

When playing literary cricket recently, hunting in the bottom of the cupboard for yellowing flannels, pads stained green from desperate dives to avoid being run out, cracked bat, box, and other essential gear, it occurred to me that 'gear' in this sense of sporting accoutrements might be a new term of jock jargon. Hunting for its origins in the bottom of the *OED*, I discovered that it was as old as Chaucer in this sense. You remember that the Cook in *The Canterbury Tales* had sharp and ready all his 'gear', including, no doubt, his box. I note also that gear used to be a slang term for the male organs of generation, and that the new British sporting term for the uniform worn by members of a team, especially a football team, is 'strip'. There is little new in sporting slang under the pavilion clock; and sporting hacks are continually resourceful in their search for synonyms for balls and other gear of mystery.

26/ TITANIC

That old sinking feeling

Yes, we arraign her! But she,
The weary Titan! with deaf
Ears, and labour-dimm'd eyes,
Regarding neither to right
Nor left, goes passively by,
Staggering on to her goal.
Matthew Arnold, *Heine's Grave*, line 87

The *Titanic* has become our byword for disaster. When the largest ship in the world went down on 15 April 1912, it was not just the great loss of life in those icy waters that aroused public pity and terror, and brought a new catchword into the language. It was, as F. L. Lucas pointed out, the tragic irony, and the uncanny coincidence that, against incalculable odds, brought together the great ship, on her maiden voyage, from the east and the iceberg from the unimaginable remoteness of the north. However, I think that our popular modern metaphor about the *Titanic* as the unsinkable that did the unthinkable has a hole below the water-line. I can find little contemporary evidence that the *Titanic* was regarded as virtually unsinkable until after she had sunk. With hindsight we have created the myth, or at any rate greatly exaggerated it, because it makes a more dramatic metaphor. We now potently and powerfully believe that the *Titanic* was hailed as unsinkable, and the subject of much ballyhoo to that effect, before her maiden and fatal voyage.

If so, one might ask why the *Olympic* did not have similar heartening claims made for her. She was almost identical to the *Titanic*, and had been in service for ten months before the *Titanic*'s maiden voyage. *The Times*, reporting the launch of the *Olympic* (21 October 1910) and her maiden voyage (14 June 1911) made much of her

109

size, the problem of launching, the luxury of accommodation, and the fact that her lower speed (21 knots) allowed her to have smaller engines than the *Mauretania* and the *Lusitania*. It was stated as a matter of statistics that she had fifteen bulkheads or watertight compartments, but the conclusion was not drawn that this made her unsinkable.

The launch of the *Titanic*, at that time the largest ship in the world, was reported in *The Times* on 1 June 1911. We remarked that she would be heavier than the *Olympic* when fitted out; but, being lighter at launch, she caused a smaller wave. When the *Titanic* sailed from Southampton on 10 April 1912, little attention was paid or comment made in the press, other than short pieces about the grandeur of the passenger-list, the comforts they would enjoy, the attractiveness of the sports facilities, and so on. Nobody was writing about unsinkability, which has become the principal characteristic of the *Titanic* for the tragic irony of subsequent generations.

There was a typical and, with hindsight, ironic example at the end of the editorial in *The Manchester Guardian* of 12 April. It was writing about the novel arrangement of the promenade deck: 'On the upper deck one can look through the windows, and, safely sheltered from contact with the outer air, obtain a full view of the sea, so much appreciated by passengers. Let us be grateful for that provision.'

Diligent search has turned up a few intimations of unsinkability before the *Titanic* sank. In May 1911 the White Star Line issued a publicity booklet in which they described their two new vessels, *Olympic* and *Titanic*: 'Each door is held in an open position by a suitable friction clutch, which can be instantly released by means of a powerful electric magnet controlled from the Captain's bridge, so that, in the event of accident, or at any time when it might be considered advisable, the Captain can, by simply moving an electric switch, instantly close the doors throughout, practically making the vessel unsinkable.'

There is some other evidence that people thought of the *Titanic* as unsinkable before she sank, but we do not know how much of it was manufactured with hindsight and irony by those who survived. Mrs Albert Caldwell survived the disaster. She reported afterwards that, while she was watching the deck hands carrying up luggage at Southampton, she asked one of them: 'Is this ship really non-sinkable?' She received a reply that echoed down the years in dramatizations of the disaster: 'Yes, lady. God himself could not sink this ship.'

110

Other irony after the event records that, when the passengers, alerted by the crew, began turning out of their cabins, one young woman remembered how she had teased a steward only four days before for putting a lifebelt in her stateroom, if the *Titanic* was really so unsinkable. She recalled the incident many years later, when the myth-building had started and may have influenced her. Major Arthur Peuchen, who survived because he was a yachtsman able to manage a lifeboat, was one of many who noticed a very slight tilt in the deck soon after the collision. He said later that he remarked on this to a friend, who replied insouciantly: 'Oh, I don't know. You cannot sink this boat.' After the first imprecise reports of an accident, the White Star offices in New York were besieged by journalists. They were reported as emitting calm confidence: 'We believe that the boat is unsinkable.'

On these flimsy foundations have we constructed our monstrous myth of unsinkability. Only after the underwater spur of ice (from an iceberg that had probably recently overturned and was showing a dark side: there was no wind or swell to create warning ripples round it) had ripped three hundred feet out of the *Titanic*'s starboard side, did the press generally start to write about invulnerability. They could recognize the potency of the irony. The word unsinkable occurs for the first time in an editorial in *The Times* on the day after the disaster: the owners had done their best to make this sort of ship unsinkable.

After the *Titanic* had gone down, the press and the two enquiries resurrected the fact that she had been built to safety flotation standards higher than required by regulations then or now, with sixteen watertight compartments, and so on. But the main concern of the press at the time was the class resentment aroused by reports that greater efforts had been made to save the lives of first-class passengers. The passengers who lost their lives included 106 women and 52 children, nearly all from the third or emigrant class. The *Daily Herald* claimed that 61 per cent of first-class passengers had been rescued, against 36 second-class, and 23 third-class.

The pathos and horror of the disaster at once turned the *Titanic* into a dramatic metaphor for disastrous paradox. To quibble about the origins of that metaphor may seem like, well, changing deckchairs on the *Titanic*. But it was only after the *Titanic* sank that we started to talk of her as virtually unsinkable.

Walter Lord, whose account of the disaster, *A Night To Remember*, is the best general account, has a persuasive theory about the deep mark that the *Titanic* has made on our folk history and language.

He sees the sinking of the *Titanic* as the symbolic end of an era, which is always a good thing for a popular historian to spot. The Edwardian Rich were a remarkably tightly knit little group, who would meet on the great liners almost as if they had planned a reunion. They monopolised not only the world's wealth but also the public eye. IMM, the international combine that controlled White Star, was in turn controlled by J. Pierpont Morgan, no less. They all knew each other and the crew. The *Titanic* was one of the last stands of wealth and high society in the centre of public attention.

The loss of the magnificent ship and her millionaire passengers somehow lowered the curtain on this way of living. It was never the same again. First the war, then income tax, made sure of that. Seventy years on, the unending sequence of disillusionment that has followed cannot be blamed on the *Titanic*, but she was the first jar. Before the *Titanic*, all was quiet. Afterwards, all was tumult. That is why, to anybody who lived at the time, the *Titanic* more than any other single event marks the end of the old days, and the beginning of a new, uneasy era. To those of us who came after, the *Titanic* has become a useful, if somewhat inaccurate, cliché.

27/ TOE-RAG

And she said, 'It's a fact the whole world knows,
That Pobbles are happier without their toes.'
Edward Lear, The Pobble Who Has No Toes

The difference between coarse and refined abuse is as the difference between
being bruised by a club, and wounded by a poisoned arrow.
Samuel Johnson, *Boswell's Life*, 11 June 1784

OK; agreed; most television is chewing gum for the eyes; and gum
that has lost its spearmint. But the telly is occasionally good for
giving one a new piece of useless information. Seated one day at
the box, watching some intellectual programme such as *Minder* or
The Sweeney (British cops-and-robbers *romans noirs*), I overheard
somebody call somebody else a toe-rag. A week or so later there
it was again: toe-rag. Whence all these toe-rags, and wherefore and
wherefrom? It is evidently a term of abuse. A rude piece of slang
from the Muvver Tongue of Cockney, would you say? All over South
London and the East End second-hand car dealers (sorry: used-car
merchandizing operatives) and others on the shady side of the law
are calling each other toe-rags, and have been picked up as local
colour by teams of television 'researchers'.

There is confusion about the etymology and meaning of the word.
I have been told by a native speaker of Cockney that it is recent
rhyming slang for 'slag', British slang for a scrubber, or a coarse
or dissipated girl or woman. The origin of 'slag' herself is not clear.
It may be an example of hemiteleia, in which a phrase of rhyming
slang is used in a shortened form (as in 'ginger' for 'ginger beer'
= 'queer'; and 'jam' for 'jam-jar' = 'car') until the original long
version is forgotten. At this point a new rhyming slang phrase is
found for the shortened form, as in 'toe-rag' for 'slag'. But no

113

convincing phrase for which 'slag' may be the shortened form has been suggested. 'Slag-heap' for 'sweep' or 'creep'?

I am not persuaded by the Cockney derivation of toe-rag, partly because I have had a considerable correspondence, particularly from Glasgow and the West of Scotland, stating that toe-rag was a common term of jocular abuse when my correspondents were young, that is to say, any time from 1900 onwards. I think we can dismiss the old British Army nickname of Toe-Rags for the Saharan tribesmen called the Tuareg as the origin of the phrase. There is an interesting New Zealand derivation. *Tua rika rika* is the Maori for a slave. Apparently the whalers on the Maoriland coast used to call each other toe-riggers or slaves as a term of Antipodean Billingsgate, and the word became toe-ragger. Thumbs down, reluctantly, for the Maori slaves, as for the Tuareg.

Eric Partridge, a New Zealander educated in Australia and the British Library reading room, has many citations from New Zealand and Australia, from 1905 on, of toe-rag as a term of contempt for a person. He also gives 'toe-ragger' as a contemptuous term for a short-sentence prisoner in an Australian jail. I dare say that the explanation is no more complicated than the rags that tramps and others of the penurious classes wrap around their toes to prevent blistering. Come to think of it, 'toe-rag' is an accurate description of the socks left in my drawer after my son Jock has dressed.

A number of wordsmiths have written to me suggesting that the word should be spelt 'tow-rag', tow being a coarse piece of wool, flax, hemp, or jute used to grease the moving parts of engines, and for mopping up grease or filth, and other less mentionable purposes. Tow was the least estimable piece of equipment in a workshop; hence the abuse. It does not seem an unreasonable metaphor to describe someone as a dirty, cheap, low-grade, filthy swab. There you are: 'swab', another textile term of abuse. One grade less rude in the scale of insult, your victim could be 'shoddy'. Tow became incorporated in the first towels.

All this I potently believe, if I close my eyes, and try hard. But may I offer a tentative alternative etymology?

It is generally agreed that, after the Monarch and the Editor of *The Times*, the most important office-holder in the United Kingdom is the President of Trinity College, Oxford. John Aubrey, that invaluable mine of gossip and inconsequential information, records that Dr Ralph Kettell (1563–1643), the famous President of Trinity who left his name to one of the College buildings, scolded the under-

114

graduates and called them a number of abusive names, including 'tarrags'. Could this be an early example of toe-rags, the vogue term that has suddenly become so popular for giving spurious verisimilitude to otherwise bald and unconvincing television programmes?

That last paragraph was a glaring example of folk etymology. The English have always been keen on this amateur activity, because it gives scope for their pedagogic and fantastic propensities. All amateur etymologists know that 'posh' meaning smart or 'classy' is derived from the initials of 'port outward, starboard home', referring to the more expensive side for cabins on ships formerly travelling between England and India. Amateur etymologists are wrong. Their charming derivation was blown out of the water by G. Chowdharay-Best's *Mariner's Mirror* in 1971, and sunk without trace by the *OED Supplement Volume III, O-Scz* in 1982.

Amateur etymologists, who are as fissiparous into sects as the early church or the extreme left in politics, have a dozen different etymologies for O.K. One school asserts that O.K. represents the Choctaw word *oke*, 'it is'. Another school derives it, with sublime dottiness, from the French *au quai*. Another derives it from a word in the West African language Wolof, brought in by slaves in the southern States of America. All these versions, according to the *OED*, lack any form of acceptable documentation; which is Lexicographese for 'amateur codswallop and malarkey.' The authoritative derivation, supported with quotations going back to 1839, is nothing more erudite than a jocular alteration of the initials of 'all correct' to 'orl korrect.' The phrase was used as a slogan and popularized by the Democrats in the American presidential election campaign of 1840. The Democratic candidate was Martin Van Buren (1782–1862). He was born at Kinderhook in New York State, and was nicknamed 'Old Kinderhook'. The O.K. Club was founded by Democrats in New York in 1840. Old Kinderhook's initials helped to bring the phrase into the lexicon. But you try telling that to amateur experts committed to another derivation.

Another charming piece of folk etymology derives 'batty', meaning away with the fairies and harmlessly insane, from Fitzherbert Batty, an eccentric barrister, who lived in Spanish Town, Jamaica, in the nineteenth century. His eccentricity became so pronounced that in 1839 he was certified insane. The case attracted considerable interest in the London press; and, according to folk etymology, Fitzherbert Batty became the eponym of 'batty'. A variation derivation explains that the original batty gentleman was William Battie (1704–76),

115

author of the *Treatise on Madness*. The psychiatrist as eponym, not the patient. Let us not go into the loose screws and fruitcakes, the lost marbles and displaced rockers, whose etymology escapes me.

Samuel Johnson, the only literary genius who was also a lexicographer, was the great folk etymologist. In his *Dictionary* he said that 'helter-skelter' was derived from an Old English expression meaning the darkness of hell. A brash young Irishman read the derivation, and exclaimed: 'That's a very far-fetched etymology.' Johnson's disciple exclaimed back, indignantly: 'Well, young sir! I suppose you can give a better etymology.' History does not record it, but I dare say he added: 'You bog-trotting toe-rag.'

Quick as a flash, the Irishman replied: 'Oh, yes sir! from the Latin; *hilariter celeriter*, merrily and swiftly; won't that do?' Quite wrong, of course; like Johnson's derivation, quite wrong. But terrific. That's folk etymology for you.

28/ WHELKS

In search of the original whelk stall

Whelk: A marine gastropod mollusc of the genus *Buccinum*, having a turbinate
shell, especially *Buccinum undatum*, common on the European and North
American coasts, much used for food.
OED

Philip Hope-Wallace of *The Guardian*, one of the great critics of
our generation, was the Master of the Misprint. His own favourite
concerned his description of Tosca as behaving like 'a tigress robbed
of her whelps.' His editor, a feminist, changed 'tigress' to 'tiger'.
The printer, on his own initiative, changed 'whelps' to 'whelks'. So
Tosca appeared 'like a tiger robbed of his whelks.'

The text in this chapter, brothers and sisters, is whelks. I can see
that this is not a lot of fun for the squeamish among us, who have
so far avoided eating the little creatures, on the grounds that extract-
ing the meat from the shell is hideously like the man on the Underground picking his ear with his little finger.

In *Enoch Arden* Tennyson could not bring himself to mention
even fish directly:

> '... and Enoch's ocean-spoil
> In ocean-smelling osier, and his face,
> Rough-redden'd with a thousand winter gales
> Not only to the market-cross were known ...'

His euphemism about ocean-spoil, alive, alive, O, provoked sardonic
Walter Bagehot to remark: 'So much has not often been made of
selling fish.'

We are less mealy-mouthed in this book. Whelks. In a column

in *The Times* in 1982 I threw out *en passant* the observation that it was a scholarly crux to discover the origin of the expression: 'He (or, for that matter, she) couldn't run a whelk stall.' This provoked my friend Henry Button to write to me from Cambridge to bring me up to date with the great whelk-hunt.

For nearly twenty years Mr Button has been looking for the original whelk-stall. He has sought it with thimbles, he has sought it with care; he has laid snares for it in the correspondence columns of *The Times*.

Until comparatively recently the earliest known sighting was in a speech by the late Gerald Nabarro to the House of Commons on 22 November 1966. Sir Gerald bellowed, with characteristic pugnacity, that he had spent his life running businesses, 'whereas the great majority of Honourable Gentlemen opposite have not the qualifications to run a whelk stall profitably.'

It caught on. The vivid phrase was at once picked up and worked to death by the leader-writing and other word-spinning classes. Feeble early variants, introduced for elegant variation and quickly dropped, were, 'incapable of managing a village sweet shop', and, 'I doubt their ability to run a profitable toffee shop.' A far jollier variant in a parliamentary sketch was, 'No doubt the Ministers are good eggs at heart, but one could not be sure of their ability to sell cut-price beer at the Durham Miners' Gala.' The whelk stall soon acquired a similar tail of qualification: 'He could not run a whelk stall on a Bank Holiday on Southend Pier.'

Lord Shawcross excited hopes in a letter to *The Times* in which he wrote: 'If (to adopt Ramsay MacDonald's famous phrase) Members have no knowledge even of the running of a whelk stall . . .' When immediately and closely questioned, he replied that he had not got the exact reference, but had long understood that the phrase was originally used, or at any rate brought to public notice, by Mr Ramsay MacDonald. Lord Shawcross wrote: 'A whelk stall, I understand, requires no great experience or efficiency in its management.' It must require a certain cold-bloodedness to shovel the little creatures into cardboard cups.

Another variant that occurs from time to time is a fish-and-chip shop, which the party of the first part is said to be incapable of running. We asked the Fishmongers' Company, and they confirmed our opinion that such a shop would be harder to run than a whelk stall.

There the fishy tail ran out. Until more whelking by Henry Button produced a revelation about the Great Whelk Stall Mystery in *The Cambridge Evening News*. This was the discovery of a remark made by John Burns in 1894, referring, as it happens, to the Social-Democratic Federation: 'From whom am I to take my marching orders—from men who fancy they are Admirable Crichtons, Pitts and Bolingbrokes, but who have not got sufficient brains and ability to run a whelk stall?'

John Burns, the labour leader and great popular orator, who gave us the Thames as 'liquid history', and 'the full round orb of the docker's tanner', would be an admirable originator of the whelk stall. The phrase still lives. It is something of a cliché, but its robust populism is irresistible to the talking and scribbling classes. Can we find an earlier citation of the phrase than John Burns's? Henry Mayhew, in *London Life and Labour*, described the whelk-men as 'the biggest rogues in Billingsgate.' But roguery is not the same as incompetence. If anybody can come up with an instance of the whelk stall catch phrase before 1894, Henry Button and I will give him— oh well, five gallons of whelks.

29/ WITCH-HUNT

Saw you the weird sisters?

Witchcraft has driven many poor people to despair, and persecuted their minds
with such buzzes of atheism and blasphemy as has made them even run distracted
with terror.
Cotton Mather, *The Wonders of the Invisible World*, 1692

Some phrases are so loaded with emotion and politics that it is
impossible to use them calmly and analytically. My text in this
chapter, brothers and sisters, is witches; in particular, the phrase
witch-hunt. We use it all the time in the inky trade; and politicians,
union leaders, and other ranters in the gassy and allied trades also
use it all the time. And yet, none of us believes that there are such
things as witches. Correction: we used to. The influential English
lawyer, William Blackstone, went so far as to lay down in his
Commentaries on the Laws of England: 'To deny the possibility, nay,
actual existence, of witchcraft and sorcery is flatly to contradict the
revealed word of God.' And in the grottier Sunday newspapers one
can sometimes read about grown men and women dancing around
churchyards, when they would be more sensibly employed wearing
some clothes and sitting at home watching even *Dallas*. I take it
that the attraction is the nudity, the notoriety, and the chance of
getting one's picture, smudged, in the paper.

Witch-hunt is always used tendentiously, and has become a serious
obstacle to clear thinking. We all know, or think we do, that there
are no such things as witches. Therefore, a *witch-hunt* is, by definition, as superfluous an activity as a hunt for a unicorn or a chimera.
Therefore, by a kind of sympathetic magic, there can be no such
things as Reds under the Beds, or, for that matter, Blues in the
Loos. Therefore, for example, to seek to secure the resignation of
120

a confessed traitor from the British Academy, or to prevent the adoption of a fascist member of the National Front as a Conservative candidate, is made to seem to indulge in a piece of cruel and long-discredited superstition.

I suppose that some of the more thoughtful who use the term might say that, historically considered, *witch-hunts* always were indiscriminate affairs, in which rumour and malice played the largest part; and that that is precisely the point that they are trying to bring out when they use the phrase. All the same, the expression half conceals such a powerful *petitio principii* that it needs to be disrobed and exposed as an ugly, silly body, like that of the prancing modern witch in a suburban churchyard.

There are no witches in the real world. But there may be people who are unfitted by their actions, or by their beliefs resulting in actions, for the posts they hold. They should be sacked, and maybe exposed as well. I know that this is offensive to the modern compassionate and 'caring' heresy that nobody should ever be sacked from anything; but there must be circumstances in which it is true.

Witch-hunt originated in American political rhetoric, as do so many of the livelier phrases of English. It referred to the notorious witch trials in Salem, Massachusetts, in the seventeenth century; and it was appropriately applied to the activities of Senator Joseph R. McCarthy, with his mysterious lists of Reds in the State Department, with numbers that grew every time that he spoke. McCarthy was as deluded and dangerous and evil as Cotton Mather, or any of the famous witch-hunters.

Witch-hunt was first applied to Communists shortly after the 1914–18 War. A. Mitchell Palmer, the Attorney General in Woodrow Wilson's administration, led what was described as a 'Red hunt', and was reported by the newspapers to be finding 'Communists under every bed', in another phrase of political rhetoric that still has mileage in it. On the eve of his election as President in 1952, Eisenhower made a campaign pledge that he would 'engage in no *witch-hunts* or character assassination.' He added that he would try 'to prevent infiltration of Communists and fellow travellers into government.'

I know that the meaning of these emotionally loaded value words of political rhetoric depends on whereabouts you are standing in the political Tower of Babel. But I do not think that the wish to rid one's administration of spies in the pay of a foreign power can

121

be described as a *witch-hunt*, in the extreme acceptance of the phrase, without some risk of terminological inexactitude.

Witch-hunt is a boo-word, to attack an attack by one's opponents on one's friends. Its opposite is a whitewash, which is an attack on an exoneration by one's opponents of their friends. And the abuse of witches as Aunt Sallies of political rhetoric is older than Joe McCarthy. *Witch-hunting* was attacked before now. There is a seventeenth-century proverb: 'They that burn you for a witch will lose their coals.'

We should not be surprised that these political words carry more evaluative passion than exact descriptive meaning, being, as the small boy said of the pelican, 'ninety per cent mouth.' That is the way of political words. Politicians, particularly of the left, tend to talk of their activities in religious metaphors (crusade, faith, This Great Movement of Ours, The Great Society), and images of revolution (struggle, battle, march, banner), rather than the boring factual terms of practical politics. That is the way to animate the apathetic masses, who have better things to think about than politics, and as a consequence to devalue political words into slogans. The real meat of politics is discussed in terms of money, votes, vested interests, practical difficulties, and so on. The sauce for the voters is made out of rousing slogans of theology, warfare, and revolution.

The most enjoyable tug-of-war over these terms of political Newspeak goes on over the most emotionally loaded and supposedly most attractive, such as Socialist and Democrat. Everybody who is anybody to the left of politics wants to wear the linguistic badges of honour of being called Socialist and Democrat. Everybody has so called herself and himself from Rosa Luxemburg to Matteoti. Historically, Social Democrat was another name for Marxist. Marx was a Social Democrat. So was Lenin. The Bolshevik Party's full name was the Russian Social Democratic Workers' Party until after the October Revolution. In the United Kingdom the middle-of-the-road, moderate, wettish-to-Liberal wing of the Labour Party has now broken away and calls itself the Social Democratic Party. None of them are Socialist. For that matter, very few members of the Labour Party are or ever have been Socialist. For what the thin red streak of meaning left in the word undoubtedly refers to is the common ownership of the means of production, distribution, and exchange. That does not stop politicians from London to Melbourne using Socialist as a strong hurray-word, or *witch-hunt* as a strong boo-word to blacken the opposition.

30/ WIZARD

The Wizard of Was

> Regard not them that have familiar spirits, neither seek after wizards, to be defiled by them.
> *Leviticus*, XIX, 31

The slang word of approval in Britain today is 'magic'. When a football side scores, they flash 'Chelsea (or whatever the name of the successful hackers and hoofers happens to be) are MAGIC' on the electronic scoreboard. As far as one can judge in these difficult matters, the new use of 'magic' as an adjective of approbation originated in Scotland in the middle 1970s, too recently to make it into the second volume *H-N* of the *OED Supplement*. Such evidence as I have indicates that it started in Glasgow, that ferocious footballing city, and spread east and south from there. You can still see the intensifying variant 'PFM' ('pure fucking magic') sprayed and painted on walls *passim* in the proximity of Ibrox and Parkhead.

'Magic' has replaced 'wizard', which the young men of the RAF and the young women of the WRAF made their all-purpose password of commendation during the last war. I do not think that anybody still says 'wizard' today, unless his slang has remained frozen in the fashion of the mess or the prep school dormitory of forty years ago.

There is an agreeable mystery about the emergence of wizard and 'wizard prang', enormously popularized by the RAF in the war, as terms of approval. It would be nice to solve it while those who remember its birth are still alive. But it is extraordinarily difficult, except in the case of technical jargon, to trace a new usage to a single pin-pointable source. Eric Partridge, whom the wise man turns to first with such puzzling questions, recorded 'a perfectly wizard week' printed in 1933. He suggested, correctly, that 'wizard' became immensely popular in the RAF between 1939 and 1945. After 1952, however, he found it little used, except by school-children and the lower middle class: 'Such things reach them after they've reached everyone else.'

So far, so good; or wizard. We can agree that wizard meaning 'great', 'bang-on', 'spiffing', 'top-hole', 'far out', or what-have-you, can be shown to antedate the war. Can we trace the origin exactly? Professor Angus McIntosh of the Middle English Dialect Project at Edinburgh University has a suggestion. As an undergraduate at Oriel College, Oxford, 1931–4, he can testify that by some time in 1932 at the latest the word 'wizard' (in the above sense) was part of the jargon of the junior common room of that college. Happily there still survive many of his contemporaries who confirm this.

The question is whether 'wizard' was imported there, say by freshmen from some school. The other question is whether 'wizard' was, to begin with, peculiar to the Oriel common room. Professor McIntosh thinks it was. No sooner had I floated this fly across the columns of *The Times* than an avalanche of letters descended from many of the colleges of Oxford and Cambridge, and from schools as temperamentally far apart as the Dragon School, Oxford, and Charterhouse, claiming priority, or at any rate contemporaneity with Oriel in the use of 'wizard'.

'Wizard' could be used in the superlative. Professor McIntosh can remember a friend describing his fiancée as 'the wizardest thing that ever trod'; a sentence that has a charmingly period ring, unmistakably of the Thirties. A use of 'wizard' in the comparative would have been unacceptable, or only barely acceptable.

Around 1933, when the glamour of 'wizard' was wearing thin, the ravers of Oriel introduced an alternative substitute, which had its brief day, but did not spread far or last long. This was the word 'king'. Oriel undergraduates would say that someone was a 'king man', or that they had had a 'king game' or a 'king meal'. It was not possible to compare 'king' in the degrees of comparative or superlative. Some derive this use from Mr Kingman, the senior college scout at Oriel at the time. Mischievous sceptics argue that 'king' was not used as an adjective, but as an abbreviation of a present participle, as in '—king good meal.' What the verb was, we can only guess.

In such pretty puzzles of language one turns next to the Oxford Dictionaries in St Giles', where the lexicographers are toiling among

124

the slips and filing cabinets on the great *OED Supplements* until the crack of doom. So far they have turned up an early 'wizard' in Rose Macaulay's *Going Abroad*, 1934: 'It *is* pretty marvellous, isn't it?' 'Simply wizard.'

'Wizard' used as a hurray-epithet also turns up in Evelyn Waugh's *Black Mischief*, Ngaio Marsh's *Surfeit of Lampreys*, Monica Dickens's *The Fancy*, and other well-known pre-war works. Item, Waugh: 'They righted themselves and stopped dead within a few feet of danger. "Wizard show that", remarked the pilot.' And here is Gilbert Frankau, the popular novelist, versifying in 1937:

'Or "wizard", as that Mayfair slang which so enriches
The Mayfair parlance designates its witches.'

Those inverted commas indicate that 'wizard' is quite a new bit of slang, to Frankau at any rate. Only in 1943 does 'wizard' appear in the classic sources of RAF slang. *It's a Piece of Cake* published in that year defined it: 'Wizard—really good, first-rate, tip-top.'

There are three more indicators of a precise date for the origin of 'wizard': the aeronautical, the American, and the comic.

First, the most glamorous aircraft at RAF air displays from 1930 onwards was the Westland Wizard. For that matter, at the same period the Rolls Royce Merlin engine powered such machines as the Vickers Supermarine Seaplane that won the Schneider Trophy. The RAF connexion is strong.

The American connexion was introduced by Commander John Irving in his little etymology *Royal Navalese*, published in 1946. In it he stated that 'wizard' was 'an adjective which has been flown from America into the Navy by the RAF. It implies that someone or something is marvellous and verging upon the miraculous.' He stated that 'wizard' was common in colloquial American usage between the wars. I can find no evidence to support this assertion, in Webster or the other obvious places. Evidence of an American source is sometimes seen in Vachel Lindsay's *Litany of the Heroes* (1918):

'God lead us past the setting of the sun
To wizard islands of august surprise.'

At about the same time on the British side of the Atlantic Edmund Gosse was writing in *The White Throat*: 'The wizard silence of the hours of dew.' Both these citations, as well as being mawkishly awful, contain examples of 'wizard' used adjectivally, combining the ideas of the miraculous and the superlative. Neither could have been written seriously if 'wizard' had by the time of writing started to acquire its 'wizard prang' connotation.

Wizards were popular characters, with their tall hats and wands, in the children's comics that found a mass market after the first war. One promising source for 'wizard' in the wizard-prang sense is the boys' story-magazine called *The Wizard*, first published in 1922. It was one of the so-called 'Big Five' story-papers that emanated from Dundee between the wars. The other four were *Adventure*, *Rover*, *Skipper*, and *Hotspur*. In its original sense the title of *The Wizard* connoted sorcerer, magician, and similar creatures that infested rival comic strips. But gradually during the Twenties and Thirties, perhaps helped by the RAF connexion, it came to be used as a superlative. It is interesting to note that in A.J. Jenkinson's survey *What Do Boys and Girls Read?*, published in 1940, *The Wizard* headed the list of favourite papers read by boys between the ages of twelve and fifteen. By 1943, a good percentage of that group would have been in the armed forces, and not a few in the RAF.

If you want to go seeking farther back for adjectival wizards, you can try Milton's *Lycidas*:

> 'Nor on the shaggy top of Mona high,
> Nor yet where Deva spreads her wisard stream.'

If you take the word here to mean 'tip-top' as well as 'enchanted', it gives you a date of 1638 for 'wizard'. But I dare say that some historian will write to me demonstrating that the Black Prince was heard to say 'Wizard show' after the battle of Poitiers.